Conversations With Top Real Estate Investors Vol. 1

With contributing Authors

Bob Snyder

Leslie Ann Betzler

Eric Counts

David Diehl

Richard & Jennifer Galarse-Pancoast

Jeff & Janet Grenier

Aaron Hammill

David Jaquish

James & Lisa Leis

Anjanette Mickelsen

Chris Neugent

Malaika Singleton

Carl & Stac'ey Volden

JC & Linda Williams

Atarah Wright

Woody Woodward

Warning—Disclaimer

The purpose of this book is to educate and inspire. This book is not intended to give advice or make promises or guarantees that anyone following the ideas, tips, suggestions, techniques or strategies will have the same results as the people listed throughout the stories contained herein. The author, publisher and distributor(s) shall have neither liability nor responsibility to anyone with respect to any loss or damage caused, or alleged to be caused, directly or indirectly by the information contained in this book.

ISBN: 978-0-9982340-0-7

Table of Contents

Introduction

Have you ever wanted to be sitting at the table when major real estate transaction were happening just to be able to glean insider information? If your answer was, "Yes" then this book is dedicated to you. You are going to be like a fly on the wall as top real estate investors are being interviewed and sharing their tips and strategies to being successful. These are honest and raw interviews with the intent to inspire you to follow your real estate dreams.

Bob Snyder

Renatus was founded and is led by 25-year entrepreneur, Mr. Bob Snyder. As CEO and President, Mr. Snyder is responsible for day-to-day company operations, affiliate marketing program expansion, course curriculum evaluation and renewal, practitioner-instructor recruiting, and month-over-month increased sales performance.

Mr. Snyder began his entrepreneurial journey over 25 years ago with the desire to leave a positive mark on the world. Establishing himself as a marketing leader, he gained first-hand knowledge of what drives marketing and team-building success. Mr. Snyder built and managed sales organizations with tens of thousands of individuals, achieved top status in multiple companies, and became a top income earner in the direct selling industry. He has freely shared his formula for success as he served on more than a dozen leadership counsels and advisory boards in the direct sales industry, received recognition in national publications as an expert in his field and has personally mentored over a dozen marketers to become seven-figure earners.

After years of building and growing marketing teams, Mr. Snyder's vision transitioned him into developing companies to expand the entrepreneurial spirit that has made this country the world's economic

1

leader. He has founded and co-founded dozens of companies that have collectively produced hundreds of millions of dollars in revenue. His real estate company completed over 2,500 real estate transactions while his former education company trained over 60,000 entrepreneurs on the subject of real estate investing and business ownership.

Contact Info:
www.MyRenatus.com

Shannon:
According to Forbes magazine, real estate is one of the top three ways that people become wealthy. As a real estate expert, why do you feel that this is the case?

Bob:
Because real estate is one of the three basic human needs: food, water, and shelter. There's always going to be a demand for real estate. Tech companies come and go, financial companies come and go, media companies come and go, but real estate is constant, and we are always going to have a need for it. Those individuals who position themselves with the right kind of properties are always going to be able to generate monthly cash flow.

Shannon:
Is that what inspired you to get into real estate: supply and demand?

Bob:
No. What inspired me to get into real estate was my wife. She dragged me kicking and screaming into real estate.

Here's the thing, I didn't understand it, and we always fear what we don't understand. I had been raised with the idea that a secure retirement required investments in the stock market. The problem was that I kept giving money to my broker and I continued to GET broker!

My wife was increasingly frustrated that we kept losing money on Wall Street, even from our conservative mutual fund investments. They weren't producing any kind of a sustainable return. By contrast, her mother and father invested in real estate while she was growing up. They made a habit of buying properties, paying them off, selling them, and buying others to build their portfolios. They developed cash flows that would take care of them in their retirement. Today, my father-in-law is eighty-eight years old and he and his wife live very comfortably from their paid-for real estate. The proof's in the pudding.

So, after losing a bunch of money on Wall Street my wife came to me and said, "Listen. We need to be in real estate. It's the way to build and secure our future and our kids' future. It's not Wall Street. It's not the stock market and it's not this other nonsense that you've been dealing with." Unfortunately, I was stubborn. I did not want to listen to her, but she was right and the last thing in the world I ever wanted was to tell her that she was right.

Shannon:

Now, looking back, you think, "Thank Goodness she was right."

Bob:

Yes, and think about what happened as a result of that, but it didn't happen overnight. She worked on me and worked on me, and I kept saying no. Then she finally came to me and she said, "Listen, Bob. I found this great little duplex. Its owner occupied on one side with a tenant on the other side, so the owner really fixed it up nice. The property is for sale by owner. We can get it a decent deal. It'll cash flow after we get a mortgage on it. You won't have to deal with it. I will manage it. I just need your support because if I don't do this I'm going to regret this rest of my life and you wouldn't want that, would you?" I mean, come on, what do you say to that?

Shannon:

You say, "You know, honey, I think we should get into real estate."

Bob:

I said, "You're absolutely right, but if this thing goes south I don't know if I'll be able to resist saying I told you so."

About a year later we were taking a look at the property's rents and depreciation schedule. All I could think was, "Holy smokes, we've got somebody living in our investment property who works all month long to make sure that we're the first one that gets paid. What an amazing business model." Then we get all these tax write offs, and the property was appreciating in value. This is phenomenal! It was one of those moments where I was like, "Wow, I'm glad I thought of it."

Shannon:

So when you were sitting in that real estate office, did she turn to you and say, "I told you so," or did she just say, "Bob, I am so glad you thought of this."

Bob:

You know, it's funny, Holly was really good about it. She just said, "You know what? You just needed to see it. You just needed to see it and do it," and she was right. All I could think to say was that we need to be doing a whole heck of a lot more of this, and that's what started our real estate investing career.

Back then we were so green, so naïve, we didn't understand real estate. We didn't understand wholesale buying opportunities. We did what 99.9 percent of the investors in this country do: go out, find a property, pay almost full price for it, put a tenant in the darn thing, and then you pray and hope that it's going to cash flow sometime in the next ten years. That's where our investing career started, but it gave me the bug and I had a desire to learn more, to grow in that business, to learn creative real estate strategies so that I could acquire properties for pennies on the dollar or buy them without any money out of pocket. I understood that with the right knowledge and drive to be a successful investor, I would never have to worry about money again.

Shannon:

Now, you've got all this knowledge and you've got years of experience, if someone wanted to get started in real estate, what would you recommend is the very first thing they do?

Bob:

The very first thing they need to do is get educated. That's just it. It's a business whereby if you know what you're doing you can make a whole lot of money and if you don't you can lose a whole lot of money. There is absolutely no ceiling on your income—the sky's the limits. You can become a millionaire, a billionaire, and I'm sure that down the road there will even be trillionaire real estate investors. The problem is, there's no floor either.

Shannon:

Yeah, I guess, if there's no ceiling...

Bob:

Yeah, if you don't know what you're doing, you can lose money. That's the biggest thing. You've got to get educated so that you have at least a common baseline of information, so you know how to fall in love with the deal and not the property. You need to know how to work the numbers and ensure that you are making a good, prudent business decision that's going to be profitable for you. The next thing is you've got to take action. I see too many individuals who fall into the category of what I call, educated derelicts. They're so versed on all sorts of different real estate strategies and different ideas, but they don't do anything with it. It's just fear that holds them back.

Shannon:

What do you do to get over that fear?

Bob:

Again, get educated. Education builds competency and when you feel competent about something you are more likely to take action. Action helps you to overcome fear, so the real formula for success is for a person to get educated and then to get busy. Education without action will not produce results.

For example, there are three types of students: the drop outs, the graduates, and the eternal. Those who keep learning and never start applying what they have learned continue to make up a larger and larger segment of our population. They are paralyzed by fear.

Let me give you an old acronym for fear

False

Evidence

Appearing

Real.

I believe that wealth is a mindset. Individuals start a conversation in their own mind that leads them to a certain belief, that belief either prevents them from moving forward or actually compels them to move forward. How they see risk plays an important role. Somewhere in their internal dialogue is a conversation about risk. When their focus shifts to all that can go wrong with an opportunity, they talk themselves out of moving forward with that opportunity.

That's why we build local communities of real estate investors all across the country. These local groups get together on a regular basis to talk about their real estate deals and what's going on in their business. When you've got somebody brand new who is fearful about fixing and flipping or building cash flow, it makes all the difference in the world to immerse them in an active community of investors. Surrounded by investors who are making offers, doing deals, and making money, a student gains confidence to make it happen for themselves.

At Renatus, we surround our students with examples of success so that they can get a realistic view of what it takes to succeed. In colleges and universities, students are stuck on the degree treadmill. They risk nothing and just keep going from class to class to class and degree to degree to degree. The lack of real world experience is the challenge with higher education.

Shannon:
Which becomes their new job.

Bob:
Yeah. It's not until they get into the real world that they start to experience anything. Believe me, I am a big proponent of education in whatever form that it can possibly come from. Unfortunately, higher education is letting more people down. They're getting degrees in fields of study that they will never make a living in and sometimes it enables them to just stay in that "safe" environment where they never take action which is why student loan debt continues to increase and student outcomes continue to decrease.

Shannon:
So, how do you change that?

Bob:

Specialized knowledge. It's unfortunate that the world of academia will never accept our type of educators because many of them don't have a college degree. Heck, some of them barely got their GED, but they are all successful, profitable investors. As for me, I got right into the world of business and by the time my friends were all graduating from college, I was making two to three times the money they were making.

Shannon:

How did you get educated? What did you do?

Bob:

You're going to love this story. I started my career in sales and marketing and then because of the frustration I dealt with working for someone else, I stepped into the wonderful world of owning and operating my own businesses. I had learned over the years how to build training platforms. I knew how to build sales teams. I knew how to create and build companies and I had a business partner who was also a seasoned entrepreneur. Together we were involved in a travel company but, after 9/11, nobody wanted to talk about travel; every-body was hunkered down and fearful of getting around the world. Our travel business really tanked. I did about everything I possibly could to get the wings back on the plane and make that thing fly again, but it just wasn't happening.

It was at that point that I had a conversation with my partner. I said, "Listen. Sometimes the best way to protect an opportunity is to create a new one." We owned real estate but we didn't understand wholesale buying or a lot about the real estate industry. I suggested we create an educational company centered on real estate investing. Then we hired the big gurus to come in and teach our people how to invest. The idea was that while our students learned, we would learn. What an idea, right?

That's where it all started. But the challenge was that the gurus we hired to teach students, students who paid good money to be in those classes, often refused to teach! They only wanted to whet the appetite of the listener so that they could up sell them to their own courses.

Shannon:

Oh, wow.

Bob:

So I talked to a friend of mine who had a PhD in Education. I told him we had a problem we needed to get beyond. Somehow we had to create a true learning environment instead of the ridiculous circus sales environment that our competitors used. He said he could help and we hired him.

He worked with us, and our staff, very closely for about a year. We brought in subject matter experts (SMEs) to help us take a good look at the real estate industry and construct our curriculum. We went out and organized focus groups from those who had paid money to gurus, both those who had and had not invested yet. All those focus groups assisted us in understanding what holds people back from investing.

We found there were four principle reasons for not investing: I don't have the time, I don't have the money/credit, I don't have the knowledge, or I'm just afraid. Those were the most common excuses. I view them as the excuses that cause failure.

Shannon:

I think we can say that for every aspect of our lives.

Bob:

Yes, we can. As soon as you start doing something, all of a sudden you say, "Hey, that wasn't so bad." I liken it to people who are W-2 employees. Most are fearful about whatever new thing they take on in life. For example, let's go back to the first day they started a new job or a new career. Were they a little intimidated? Were they a little nervous? If they're honest, they're always going to say yes. Fast forward six months. By then they have a pretty good handle on it. Most would say that they had gotten really good at their job and feel confident in it. The challenge is that they rarely ever feel like they are getting paid what they are worth?

We all go through that process. Fear is overcome through action.

We've got to get people in an environment that helps them to take one step after another. That's another thing I learned from Dr. Paul Ripicke. He taught us about the Instructional System design (ISD) methodology for curriculum building. It's what every major college and university in the country uses to build their curriculum paths and focus on student outcomes.

We thought, "well, if Harvard and Yale and Princeton are using this, we can use it too," so we went out and worked with individuals who were actual full-time investors in a specific strategy and we brought them on board. We worked with them to help us craft these classes, and then we taught them how to teach, and then we fired all the gurus. From that point forward, we had real-life investors standing up in front of our classrooms teaching our students. We forbid any of those instructors to ever sell anything in class because we knew that that would be a massive conflict of interest because the minute they started selling they would stop teaching.

Shannon:

Was there one type of person or personality that seemed to be most drawn to your classes or had the type of personality to be the most successful?

Bob:

It's not the personality, it's the circumstance. That's the one thing that all of our students shared; there was a heightened level of dissatisfaction with where they were. It didn't matter whether they were in a successful profession or they were just out of college struggling to make ends meet. They all had a level of dissatisfaction, whether it was enough time with their family, or a good enough future, or they were just sick and tired of working for a boss that didn't appreciate them. They all had a level of dissatisfaction. Again, wealth is a mindset. We just needed to give them hope.

Even for the staff who work here at Renatus, there's a huge shift in their mental framework. They may come in believing they need to contribute each month to their 401(k), but they end up learning how to do creative real estate investing to build their own wealth that they can control. It's pretty exciting to see that the staff members are also embracing the classes and getting out and doing their own deals.

Shannon:

It's kind of exciting because your employees could turn into full-time real estate investors and then you get to hire new employees and teach them, wouldn't you think?

Bob:

You know, there's always that thought in the back of your mind that, key people are going to start making so much money they're going to leave you. I encourage it, but over and over and over again I've got that same group of people who say, "You know what? This is what I want to do for the rest of my life," Renatus is a cause more than it is a job to them because they see the benefits that are showing up in other people's lives and that gives them a great deal of self-satisfaction.

Shannon:

Do you think students should find one real estate investing strategy and stick with that and become an expert, or do you think they should diversify?

Bob:

One of our favorite classes is understanding your investor ID because everybody's different. For example, some individuals have no problem going out there and buying property that they're going to put lower-income tenants into. They're just happy to get that check from the government every single month. Other individuals believe that if they wouldn't live in it, then they won't own it. We have different types of personalities and mindsets. They can all make money in real estate.

What we've got to do is figure out what their investor ID is: do they want quick turn real estate for lump sum cash returns or do they want to build cash flow over time with a nice, passive income from the property? I always tell people, once you figure out your investor ID, then you learn everything you possibly can about that strategy and you focus on that to become an expert.

But, you never stay stuck with just one strategy because markets shift and change. That's why we teach so many different strategies in Renatus. No matter what is happening with the market, no matter what is happening with the economy, if there's a shift or an adjustment in the real estate business and you haven't secured yourself with an understanding of different ways to get the same thing done, you're going to find yourself on the outside looking in and saying, "Well, gee, the economy's bad, so, the opportunity's gone." Not true, my educated students crushed it through the Great Recession. They made money hand over fist while everybody else was bellyaching and moaning that there wasn't an opportunity out there.

Shannon:

Do you have personally a favorite acquisition strategy? Which strategy just makes you the most excited?

Bob:

You know what, I love subject to, but this strategy died during the recession because equity went away and home owners owed more than the property was worth. When I started Renatus, over five years ago, I created a three-hour training series called "Fast Track to Financial Freedom." I showed individuals exactly what was going on in the marketplace, how they could capitalize on what was taking place at that time with real estate investing, and shared with them that we were about 5.2 million homes short of where we needed to be as a nation just to maintain the demand of housing for the increased population.

Many builders do not build in a recession; some went out of business and would need to ramp back up. This would not be an immediate fix. By the time you find raw land, go through all the entitlements, sometimes dealing with the city, and put a foundation in and start putting sticks up to frame the house, you're eighteen to twenty-four months out. It's not like this is just an immediate fix. You don't go, "Oh, there's a demand. I think I'll build a house here." It's going to take a while. I believed that once we got to the backside of the recession, there would be a great housing shortage and that housing shortage would create a massive adjustment in appreciation.

The good news is that the subject to real estate market has come back as prices have increased; we've seen a wild swing. Subject to is a great strategy because it's one of the best ways to acquire multiple properties and not be limited by banks and financial institutions. If you're dependent on conventional lending, you're going to be very, very limited in the amount of real estate you can do and the types of real estate transactions you can do. That's why I love a subject to–it's a great no money down strategy.

Shannon:
What about seller financing? If you're not relying on the banks, are seller financing and subject to the same thing?

Bob:
Well, yes and no. Some might refer to it as another form of seller financing because you are keeping the existing mortgage in place. Generally, seller financing is when a homeowner has a large equity position and they have the ability to create terms for the buyer to make the purchase.

Subject to is when you get the deed to the property, and you become the owner. It's yours. You own it subject to the existing mortgage, but the mortgage still stays in the name of the seller and they stay on the mortgage while you now own and control the home. Now, obviously, you've got to make sure that those payments are made, otherwise the lender will foreclose on the home and even though you're the new owner, they'll take it away from you just like they would have taken it away from the previous owner.

Shannon:
Is a subject to extremely risky as opposed to a standard seller finance, or are they about the same?

Bob:
Oh, no. When we discuss risk we have to think of who's at risk? The seller or the buyer? Individuals looking at selling their home using a subject to' are really in some serious financial stress and they know

that a foreclosure on their credit rating weighs heavier against them than bankruptcy.

Individuals that are stuck in that kind of a situation want to solve that problem before that property goes to auction and the foreclosure is complete. A smart investor will reinstate the loan and purchase the property subject to the existing mortgage. That way, a subject to helps the seller get back on track as far as reestablishing their credit, and it just takes a huge weight off of them. All the stress, all the burden, all the phone calls, all the challenges. It just takes it away so they can get a fresh start and go out and do their thing. The downside for the seller is what happens if the investor who bought the property doesn't make the mortgage payments.

Shannon:
That was my next question.

Bob:
Yep. What happens? Is there a risk? Well, absolutely there's a risk because then that seller could find themselves right back in foreclosure again. Of course, it's no different than the mess they were in to begin with so they're kind of back in the same position. But the bottom line is no investor that is really worth their salt is going to buy a property, put money into that property, and then lose that property because they aren't willing to make the payments. There's a level of assurance that everything's going to happen the way that it should happen.

Now as to the risk to the investor, it's pretty small. Worst case scenario you just walk away from the deal or give it back to the original seller and, if you haven't put any improvements into the property, you're not out anything. If you had put improvements in the property and for some reason you don't have the money to make those monthly mortgage payments, well, then shame on you, you're going to lose the money that you put into the property. Of course, an educated investor would just rent the dang thing out. Then you get a tenant making the mortgage payments for you. There's always a way if you know what you're doing.

Shannon:
That feeds back to all the different strategies. If I, as an investor, were to be in a tough spot and I had learned everything I could learn from you, it seems like I could go to my investment group and say, "Hey, who wants this property? I need help," and they would have the knowledge to help me out.

Bob:
Yep. Absolutely. You know it's just nice to have people that have been there, done that, to be able to pick their brain and lean on them from time to time. We've developed a really unique culture inside of Renatus. It's a culture of servant leadership, meaning that you never, ever ask anybody to do something you wouldn't be willing to do yourself.

If somebody in the community needs help and assistance then we have a pay it forward kind of mentality; but what I see from an awful lot of real estate groups out there, especially a lot of real estate groups, is that they're very motivated to try and maximize their relationships inside the club. There's so many investors in those things that are just looking to prey on brand new investors. They tell them they have a fantastic property that they could turn around and rehab and sell and make 50 grand, but they have to hand over a $10,000 assignment fee to get it.

Then, the brand new greenie goes and buys the property because some seasoned guy said it was going to be a great deal, and they find out that the price they bought it for was over-inflated, the supposed selling price was also over-inflated, and now they're going to lose money on the deal because they didn't know how to work the numbers for themselves. In our community, we apply a lot of emphasis on our leaders and on others in the company to make sure that we take care of community members because they're going to be with us for life.

With that continued emphasis, I outline for them how a deal should be done: Do not sell property to people in the community, unless we want to become a business partner with them, form an LLC with an operating agreement, and have exit strategies already spelled out; do not loan money to anybody in the community or borrow money from anybody in the community unless you become business partners, again with an operating agreement.

That helps to minimize risk. I hate organizations whereby brand new, especially green or naïve individuals get taken advantage of because they think that somebody is trustworthy. You must do your own due diligence because no one is going to care about your financial wellbeing as much as you.

Shannon:

You know, that is so unique to your organization and I love it. If more people just lived their life that way, not just in real estate but just lived their life that way, our world would be so incredibly different.

Bob:

We are all about student outcomes. When somebody buys an educational package from us, after the first year, if they're in good standing with the company, we convert them over to complimentary lifetime access. That means that they're going to have access to refreshed or improved and updated classes given to them for free, for life.

If we have new classes and new material that we roll out to the field, we just give it to our students, again without any additional charge. The complimentary lifetime access is a very, very coveted feature of the Renatus educational system.

Shannon:

You've done a lot of amazing things. You've built businesses, you've adapted, you're married, you have children, you have thousands of people that you mentor and that look up to you every day. What type of legacy to you want to make sure that you leave for them?

Bob:

Let me explain my motivation. The reason why I tick the way I tick, and believe me it's taken a lot of self-evaluation to figure it out, is that when I was a kid I had a father who was an alcoholic and a drug addict. His addictions created an enormous amount of financial stress in the home because we didn't know where our next meal was going to come from or what we would do when the power was turned off. I remember the bishop of our church was kind enough, when we lived behind him, to run an extension cord from his house over to our house so that we could run the refrigerator and watch Saturday morning cartoons after the power and the utilities had been turned off.

There was a lot of financial stress. I was a little kid and I didn't really understand it at that point, but as I started to grow it became more evident. The best thing that ever happened to Dad and the family was when he got caught for check fraud. That's what happens with addicts. They lie, they steal and they cheat, so that they can feed their addiction. Best thing that ever happened to him was he went away to jail for two years. Prison was a forced rehab for him.

When he was sober my Dad was a pretty brilliant guy. He graduated top of his class from University of Pennsylvania, and he went on to get his law degree from there. He was an assistant district attorney in San Francisco and had his own private practice up in Seattle. I mean, he was a smart guy. It was just addiction had taken a toll.

The other thing that meant a lot to me was my church, my faith. I served a two-year mission for my church. I loved every minute of it, being able to teach people how to apply gospel principles to bring them a lot of joy and happiness was rewarding. When you take that kind of philosophy and those correct principles and you put them into business with an investment like real estate, you can teach people a career path that will give them security, stability, financial freedom, and independence. You allow them to then give back to the community and to the world, and you can leave your kids and grandkids a lasting legacy from the inheritance they'll receive when you finally finish your time on this planet.

For me, all of that really has kind of led me to where I'm at today. My greatest satisfaction comes from seeing our students actually do what we teach them how to do and succeed. It comes from seeing them be good stewards of the money that they make. That's another thing, I'm not one of these flashy guys. I've got a nice house and I've got some nice cars, but I'm not driving around in a million-dollar Lamborghini.

There's not a lot of the flash and the bling and the nonsense with me because I don't want to set a bad example for my team. I would rather talk to them about cash flow. I would rather talk about assets. I would rather talk about balance sheets and profit and loss statements and how they can improve their lives and what they're doing to improve the lives of others. If I can make an impact on the community that really transforms their way of thinking so that they act and behave in that manner, we'll change the world.

What brings me the greatest amount of happiness is that I love seeing the positive changes in people's lives. In my first real estate company I dealt with a business partner who lost his focus. His ego got out of hand and he forgot about the people. It was all about his ego and his own self-aggrandizement. His world got so big that he just found himself working harder and harder to feed the monster of his creation. He had an enormous house and expensive cars and private servants and nannies and security details. He even had a jet.

I was just so disappointed with him; he set a bad example for the team. A lot of people in the community wanted to be like him. They started to make really bad financial decisions and leverage themselves into cars and houses and things that weren't producing income for them. He ended up filing for bankruptcy and had to liquidate millions in personal debt.

But life was always good for me because I've always lived well below my means. There's a massive lesson in that. Be a good steward of what you've got, live below your means, and you can still enjoy life, and I do. I enjoy life, and I don't have financial stress, and if everything but my real estate was taken away from me today I would still make a really nice income and never have to worry about money the rest of my life. I want people to have what I have. That's why I do what I do.

Leslie Betzler

Leslie Betzler had spent most of her life in Southeast Michigan. It was there where she raised her three wonderful children and discovered her passion for real estate. After her children completed their education, Leslie began to think about moving to Arizona. Once she made the decision, she relocated to the Phoenix metro area, where her real estate career sprouted wings and began to soar. A natural at customer service, she was able to infuse her skills with her passion and became a sought after real estate investor, as well as a licensed realtor. While working diligently to build her real estate portfolio, Leslie has joined a solid, nationally recognized real estate investment group, and has also tackled projects on her own. She also partners with her mentors and other investors on projects when the deals make sense. Leslie continues to broaden her knowledge through continuing education and stays up-to-date with current market trends.

Contact Info
Leslie Betzler
lesliebetzler@gmail.com
HomeSmart Realtor

Shannon:
What inspired you to get into real estate?

Leslie:
Believe it or not, real estate just fell into my lap. I was living in Michigan and had gotten divorced. I was $40,000 in debt, I spent days trying to figure out what I was going to do. My kids were 12, 10, and 8 at the time.

As I looked around me the only successful people I knew where investors in real estate. I started researching online on how to get into the industry. Thinking of the future I knew I was going to retire somewhere warm. I hated the cold winters. I was waiting for my last son to graduate from high school and then I was going to move to a warmer climate. The kids were either going to come with me or they were going to stay in the house which I would keep for them in Michigan, while I went and did what I needed to do for me.

All of a sudden a light bulb came on and I thought, "I need to start searching where the markets crashed, buy a home there now, and maintain it somehow." I knew it would kill me if I waited three years to buy, then paying a higher price.

I was trying to decide between the Carolinas, Florida, Las Vegas, and Phoenix. There was no way I was moving teenagers to Vegas and there was no way I was going to deal with humidity in the other two states. So, I ended up in Phoenix.

I ended up finding a great buy and hold because my realtor ended up wanting to rent it. It gave me cash flow right away and then that light bulb went on again. I realized that I could make money right away and I ended up buying a couple more homes. I put enough money together to have three buy and holds by the time I moved here in 2014.

Shannon:
Do you have a favorite type of investment?

Leslie:
Now that I've moved in here and I've gotten into investing full time, my direction has changed. I really thought that I was going to do all fix and flips.

I am working on that but I am primarily doing hard money lending. I pulled all the equity that I had in my houses and that's what I'm actually doing more than anything else right now.

Shannon:

Do you prefer hard or soft money lending?

Leslie:

I prefer hands down soft money lenders to work with.

Shannon:

If somebody came to you and said that they wanted to get started in real estate investing, what would you recommend they do?

Leslie:

I would tell them to start showing up to real estate events. Start getting to know the people there and start building relationships with the people that are going to get you to where you want to be. That's actually what I did. I started building relationships with them and now they have taken me under their wings and have started to mentor me. I've done that with a lot of people. With my work ethic people are willing to work with me.

I have skill sets that they lack. They have skill sets that I lack. To be on a team and work together we're both going to benefit. You should always look for the win/win. You've got to find the best fit for you.

Shannon:

What is the best piece of advice that anyone in real estate has given you?

Leslie:

Study the particular market in which you want to start. Understand there is risk involved. Educate yourself as much as possible. Make a decision and move forward.

I don't like people blaming others for the choices I've made. People can guide you and give you direction but the bottom line is your choice, bad or good. I like to give people credit for sending me in the right direction. There have been plenty of times that people sent me in a direction that didn't work for me. I don't blame the person that sent me. It just wasn't a good fit for me.

Shannon:
What is the best piece of advice that you have ever given to anyone that you have mentored?

Leslie:
Go with your intuition.

Shannon:
Do you think it's necessary for someone to have a good mentor or do you think they can be successful on their own?

Leslie:
They can be successful on their own. They don't need a good mentor. They can do all their own research and they can build all their own relationships. But breaking into this business is really hard without having somebody that has been in it for a while. As a newbie, you have so much ground work to do. You have to have a good reputation, and you have to have been in the industry for years to get into this part of the business. Otherwise, you're paying prices that you don't need to be paying.

If you meet a good mentor and you're at least teamed up with a good mentor, it's going to take down a lot of walls for you at the very beginning.

My thought is, this group that I'm teamed up with, I'm going to stick with them for a couple of years, then I'll have my own backing and I'll learn a lot from them and then I'm going to branch out on my own. We know that down the road we are going to outgrow each other. Right now, it's the best fit for me because it's one of three areas I'm trying to master.

Shannon:
What's one of the top real estate strategies that you have learned since you've been acquiring more education?

Leslie:

Making sure you do your due diligence and your research. Making sure you do your homework, on the people that you're working with, which is huge. Because if you come on with the wrong person, it goes south extremely fast. Not only does it have an effect on that person's reputation, but you've had a lot of contact with this person and everyone considers you part of a team. That's the thing, you've got to do your homework on who you choose to team up with.

When I am going to be investing with somebody, I make sure that their company is very, very solid. How long have they been in business? Are they honest? Are they reputable? They should have the same information about me.

Shannon:

What do you think the number one mistake is that people make when they're buying their first investment property?

Leslie:

Their number one mistake is not knowing their numbers and buying too high. The next mistake is buying in the wrong neighborhood.

Shannon:

Do you have an extensive checklist that you go through when you're looking for a property?

Leslie:

Yes, yes, very extensive.

Shannon:

Do you think that success in real estate investing is dependent on a strong economy?

Leslie:

No, it doesn't have to be a strong economy. You just have to know what you're doing. You have to buy at the right price. Buying correctly is probably the biggest, most important thing that you can do.

Shannon:

In a weak economy, what is your strongest investment strategy?

Leslie:

I would suggest the buy and hold method. You can acquire properties at a lower price. When the economy is down it usually means it's a good time for rentals.

Shannon:

In a strong economy, what is your strongest investment strategy?

Leslie:

Do not over extend yourself. Always expect market to fluctuate so invest with more than one exit strategy in mind. Don't put all your marbles in one basket.

Shannon:

What advice would you give to someone who is allowing fear to hold them back from investing?

Leslie:

The best way to conquer your fear is to jump in.

Shannon:

What are some ways that you like to use to acquire properties?

Leslie:

First, you've got to find them by getting creative. I put up signs, drive to find vacant homes, get the addresses and search for the owners.

Basically you're contacting them about a situation that they probably don't want to talk about. First you've got to win them over so they open up to you at all. You usually have to build some kind of rapport. Hopefully within the first couple of times, the conversation will open itself up and then you can ask them what's actually going on? What's the situation? This is what I do for a living, is there any way I can help you out? There's a couple of different strategies that could work for you. You just sort of open that door.

It's a long drawn out process to possibly get a property. There's a lot of shooting bullets that hit nothing. Any relationship you build with anyone is never a waste of time. Eventually things turn around and come back and bless you.

I also like to use wholesalers. I have built a lot of relationships with a lot of good wholesalers. I don't want to be just another name on a wholesaler's list. I want to get to know their people. It's all about building relationships. Make the relationships that you need in order to get in with a good wholesaler and maintain them. Give and take.

Shannon:
Why does this relationship work so well? The investor/wholesaler relationship?

Leslie:
Well, it's a win for me because I get to buy properties at a lesser cost. A good wholesaler builds a relationship with the person that's selling the property so that people are willing to talk to them and work with them.

When people are in distress about their finances, or they've had a fire or any other number of stressors, just letting them understand that we can help them out of their problems and they can walk away is a HUGE win.

Wholesaling is actually finding properties that are in distress for many different reasons. It could be financial, personal, there could be a passing of somebody; You're finding someone that's in a distressed situation and you're just trying to find a way to help them get out of it.

Shannon:
Why do most millionaires have commercial properties in their investment portfolio?

Leslie:
Most millionaires understand that buying commercial properties are for long term wealth generation. It is viewed as one building with many sources of positive cash flow coming in monthly.

Shannon:
What is the standard length of time to close a short sale?

Leslie:
This depends on several factors, one of which is the specific lending institution involved in this process. In my experience, these types of transactions are anything but short.

Shannon:
What advice would you give to someone who has poor credit or has no money and wants to get into real estate investing?

Leslie:
Wholesaling is the way the majority start in real estate when they have no money. There are ways to fix and flip with borrowing money, but you just have to do your numbers. You have to do your due diligence. You have to get educated.

Shannon:
Do you have advice for people about what they should budget for wiggle room on a rehab?

Leslie:
I always factor in about 10% more than what I plan for my rehab. Say your rehab cost is $20,000. You'd better figure in at least $2,000 for wiggle room. You never know what is going to happen when you open the walls.

Shannon:
What advice would you give someone who is just getting started?

Leslie:
If you're going to get into this business I would suggest getting a mentor, you go after the mentor who represents where you want to be in five years. If you want to be that person in five years, then that's the person you need to be following. I was really picky and

choosy on who I was deciding to mentor with.

Being with the wrong mentor is not beneficial to you at all.

Shannon:
What are three different scenarios that you have found yourself in while purchasing rental properties?

Leslie:
The very first one I bought had a lot of extensive work I had to do. The second one I bought knowing I was going to do with it so I did the bare minimum. I did have to do some rehab to get it up to standards but that one I put very little in. The last one I brought from an investor before it went on the MLS.

Shannon:
How has real estate investing changed your life?

Leslie:
It has allowed me to work for myself. I see no limit on the wealth you can achieve if you're willing to do the work.

Shannon:
What type of legacy do you want to leave behind?

Leslie:
What I want people to say is that she was a kind, giving, positive person. She lived life to the fullest.

Eric Counts

Eric Counts is an author, business trainer, and nationally featured speaker. His extensive knowledge of credit and credit repair have gained him audiences with the likes of Wells Fargo, Regions Bank, and Century 21 branches across the country. Eric has served as expert witness to lawmakers in matters of credit and debt collection, and due to his extensive knowledge of the laws governing the credit industry, Eric is considered a valuable resource by many business professionals nationwide.

Contact Info:
www.creditnerds.com

Shannon:

According to Forbes Magazine, real estate is one of the top 3 ways people become wealthy. As a real estate expert, why do you feel this is the case?

Eric:

Real estate is by far one of the safest investments. There's an old phrase, "It's the one thing they're not making any more of." Then, when people understand how to utilize real estate to grow and shelter wealth, that's when a true wealth building process can begin as opposed to putting your money away in banks or even in a 401(k). You're trying to gamble with the stock market and on something you have no comprehension of. A person who really learns and under-stands real estate—the risk drops significantly. There's always risk in any investment, but in real estate, the risk is mitigated by a solid education, because they're learning what they're doing and how to do it properly. When they do that, that's when real wealth can start to be accumulated, and you can see that in that number. It's one of the top 3 ways to become wealthy.

Shannon:

What if you have all your money in real estate and the economy crashes?

Eric:

The thing people forget, the thing people miss when they start to throw all their money at real estate is, they skip the education. We don't become a doctor without going through years and years of medical school. We don't become an attorney without going through years and years of law school. We don't become most things without going through some type of education and some type of training, and yet people will jump out and say, "I'm a real estate investor!" They throw all their money at properties, and they don't understand what they're doing. When you say things like, "Oh, real estate is so risky. What if the economy crashes?" Most of the really successful real estate investors out there have protections for themselves in place.

There's different types of real estate investing than just flipping. When you have those storms and you have your investments set up properly, you can weather those storms. I'm not saying you're going to make as much those years, but you don't have to necessarily collapse, either.

Shannon:

You have a very successful credit repair business. Is that fair to say?

Eric:

Oh, absolutely. Some people hide from the word 'credit repair' because it has such a negative connotation, but when it's done properly, legally, ethically, morally, then we don't hide from the word. Of course—yeah, we're a credit repair company. We just don't do things the way that a lot of those other companies do.

Shannon:

What inspired you to take your life, that was already so fulfilling, and decide to be a real estate investor on top of an already lucrative career?

Eric:

The answer to that one is actually really easy.

I was doing great, and the problem a lot of people have is that they look at a real estate investment as a place to make money, and yes, that exists. You find a great deal, you put together the money, you put together the resources. And you put together the cost analysis. You actually figure out if it's a good deal or a bad deal. Then you do the deal, and you make some money. That's great, but what I see real estate investment as, is if a person is already making money and they're already doing well financially, they have to have a vehicle to store that money. We don't take money and just throw it in the bank and let it sit and do nothing. Your money has to work for you. If you're not putting your money to work for you, you can make all you want. It's not really about how much you make. It's about how much you keep.

You have to protect the wealth you're able to create; however, you generate that wealth. There's lots of doctors out there and dentists out there and lawyers out there and lots of people that do well and make a lot of money. Other business owners of different types of businesses can make good money too, but they have to have a place to put that money.

Shannon:

When you decided that you needed a "place" for your money, did you look at other options for investing?

Eric:

I did. I looked at gold. I'm not going to say I'm not a fan of gold. It's a great hard asset. I looked at trading too, which is something I knew nothing about.

That was actually the hard part for me... I knew nothing about stocks. I also knew nothing about the trading process. What am I going to do? Jump right in and just, "Oh, now I'm a stock day trader?" It doesn't really make any sense. I don't understand the concept of being something that you know nothing about.

When I looked at real estate, and then when I found the real estate education company I work with, when I found that, even then I went through... classes before, so I have to say: learn what you're doing before you just jump right in. The people that are successful in real estate investment are the people who have taken the time to learn to do it right.

You know me—I always do it right. I actually went full in. I want to know everything about everything. You learn about things like unconscious incompetence, conscious competence. You know what I'm talking about? Where you don't know what you don't know, and you do know what you don't know, and you know what you know, and you don't know what you know. Does that make sense to you? I know that's a lot of knowing in there.

If I was going to sum it up, it would be, so if you don't know something, then you have no reason to ask that question. I didn't know what I didn't know.

Shannon:

You've been working to help get real estate investors' credit rebuilt for years. Did that give you more confidence?

Eric:

Actually, quite the opposite. When it came to investment, there were things I didn't know, and I knew that I didn't know them. I didn't know the best way to complete a short sale. I didn't know the best way to do these different transactions, and I knew that. What scared me more was the information I didn't know that I didn't know.

Shannon:

How did you deal with that fear?

Eric:

The same way I have dealt with all of my fears. I learn first. The more you know, the less you have to fear. Just like with my credit repair company... we took on somewhere between 75 to 100 customers. I used the word "customers" there. I should have said, "We took on 75 to 100, 'people' for free," when we started our company to learn.

We wanted to make sure that we were able to provide what we said we were going to provide. Before I started this business, I had taken a job. I was working with a friend who was a Realtor, and I was just actually helping him do some flips. When I say "helping," I mean tearing up tile and pulling cabinets down. I was labor. And I would see him make this great money. Then I would look back and remember that he paid me 100 bucks to pull down the cabinets, walls, countertops, and tile. I was working a hard day's work. He got a phone call, and it was a credit repair company, looking for somebody to do sales in the area. My friend said, "Well, you know, I wouldn't be interested in that, but my buddy, he might be interested in that." I said, "Absolutely. I need a job." I needed work. I needed anything that provided some sort of income.

I was a salesman. I went out and I was like, "All right. I'm going to sell this to everybody I can find." Well you know— it's sales. The first place you go... I sold it to my mom. I sold it to my aunts and uncles and cousins and friends and family and people in the community who knew me. Thankfully, it was a small town. There was still what we would consider prominent people in the community, business owners and landowners in the community. Within a few months, I realized that all of those people were getting ripped off by this company. They weren't providing the service they said that they were going to.

This was very hard for me to grasp. It was extremely difficult for me on a personal level because I try to live by the rules. I knew that I had to do something. If you help somebody, they will tell 3 or 4 of their closest friends. If you rip somebody off, they will tell every person they've ever met ever.

It's just our society. People share bad news so much more than they share good news. It was just something I didn't really want to live with hanging over me. I went around to all those people I could find, and I apologized. I told them, "I can't give you your money back." I only made a $50 commission per sale.

"I can't even give you the $50 back, because I've been feeding my family. I can't." I was basically working and providing for my family.

I said, "What I will do is, I'll try to provide you the service that you bought. I'll try to do my best to provide that to you." I began learning, and I jumped online, and there was so much bad information online about credit and all these myths. There's so many people selling all these e-books and selling all these courses and all of these things. I bought so many different books and things. What I learned was that they just let you put anything you want on the internet. You can just put anything on there! You can make up whatever you want, put it on Wikipedia, and it becomes fact.

From that day forward, I decided that the only information I would accept was direct from the law, direct from FICO, direct from the bureaus, direct from the Federal Trade Commission, direct from the Attorney General's Office. It doesn't mean that I would not learn from other sources, but if I learn something from another source, I would immediately go and verify that information directly with the source. I would go to the book, go to the law and say, "Is that what the law really says?" By doing that, we were able to provide a really great service to our customers, and we started getting phone calls.

"Hey, are you the guy helping people with their credit?"

"Yeah, that's me."

"Can you help me?"

I would say, "Yes, I guess so," because at the time, I had an employee mindset, a labor mindset. I didn't even understand the opportunity that was happening to me. I would say, "Yeah, I guess so."

Before long, I was working constantly for free. I was just helping all of these people. I got a call one fateful day, and the voice on the other end said, "Are you the guy helping people with their credit?" I said, "Yes, I am." She said, "How much does that cost?"

Shannon:
How did you come up with your company name?

Eric:
When I first started my business, a lot of the companies out there were trying to seem really over-professional. They were trying to seem like they were law firms or they were trying to seem like they're financial analysis or just they're trying to be more than what they are.

When we came around that, I said, "You know what? These people are already in a tough enough situation. Why do I want to put them in more stress, thinking they're walking into an attorney's office? Why do I want to put them in more stress, feeling like they're somewhere that's tough?" Instead, we came at it from a place of almost fun. Our original slogan was, "Bad credit isn't funny." Our ads were funny. We would put out a funny dog. It was a dog riding a skateboard thing and it said, "Dogs riding skateboards are funny. Bad credit isn't." It was just these funny pictures. It was these strange things. One of them was an older man in a really small t-shirt, flexing. He was an older man, but he had muscles, we had a credit score tattooed on his arm.

This was back in 2009, and we didn't want to be that over-professional, stuffy environment. Instead, we wanted to make it fun. Kind of like the Geek Squad from Best Buy.

We thought, "That's who you want to go to. If my computer is broken, that's who I want to go to, the geek."

We decided to go with Credit Nerds. When you're in school, and you need help with your math, get a nerd. That's who you get. That's where you need the help. We went with Credit Nerds, and it really took off. We've taken from a one-room office in a small town in

Arkansas to flying across the country, literally. We've even helped clients in Canada, and we've helped a few clients out in Puerto Rico and every other state.

Shannon:

Wow. That's awesome. When you look back at the part of your life when you were ripping out cabinets and tearing up tile, and your wife was waiting tables, and you look at your life today, what do you feel?

I could ask you how it has changed your life, but just from a financial standpoint, we can all see how it's changed your life. What do you feel? What is the most important feeling you have for everything you've attained?

Eric:

The funny thing about that, Shannon, is if somebody were to say, "Are you happier now?" I would say "no." I'm as happy as I was before, but I was a pretty happy guy. I've always been an optimist, so to speak.

I think that's part of why some of the opportunities that arose for me did, because I have always had a positive mindset. I always assumed that my life would work out. I always assumed that it was just a rough time. As long as I had my family, my wife, a child or 2, 2 actually, we have 2 children, then I was content. I look back at that, and it would be a big piece of advice I'd have for people: don't ever be content. I could have been able to provide for my family a lot better sooner, had I just not been content. I was content with having my family and content with having just enough. My wife and I, we fought a lot more than we do now.

I'm not saying that we don't have the occasional word. We wouldn't be a marriage if we didn't. There's not so much stress. There's not so much pressure now. When you're not fighting about money, there's so few things left to fight about.

To answer your question simply, life is a lot easier now. Not better, just easier.

If a person doesn't have the mindset to grow and keep wealth already, then they might make a little money, but they probably won't keep it, and they definitely won't continue to grow it.

Do you have an acquisition or exit strategy you're most attracted to?

Eric:

If a person has a specific exit strategy or specific strategy they're most inclined to, that's fantastic. I don't discount that in the slightest. However, in my thoughts, it's not really about what you want to do. It's about where the property sits. If you pick up to do a wholesale deal and the wholesale doesn't work, maybe you flip it yourself. Then if the flip isn't quite the right strategy for it, then you hold it, and then maybe you become the bank and lend on it. One of the things I learned from Scott Rowe was it's important to be able to be what they call a transactional engineer. It's not about what you want to do. It's about what works best for the property and how the property works best, to coin a phrase.

If you're looking into it saying, "Okay, I want to flip. I'm going to flip. I'm going to flip. I'm going to flip," and then you get a property and that property just doesn't... It just doesn't fit for a good flip, you have to be able to say, "Okay, you know what? I'm not going to flip this one. I'm going to hold this one for a little while," or, "I'm going to do this," or, "I'm going to do that." Whatever that may be. I might provide a lease option on it. I might do who knows what with it. My biggest piece of advice for that question really would be to not limit yourself to one transaction. Don't limit yourself to one type of thing.

We can all have a favorite, but really make sure you understand how to manage those properties because if you only really focus on or know one strategy, then you're going to get caught. You're going to get caught holding the bag. Because if that property isn't a good fit for that strategy, that's where people lose. They think, "Oh man, this thing didn't work. Real estate doesn't work." It works, but they just didn't know what to do with it.

Shannon:

What is one of the biggest mistakes investors make when buying their first property?

Eric:

One of the number one mistakes I feel like people always make in real estate investing is they become so emotionally attached to their original plan or the original property.

I have no emotional attachment to any strategy or any property or anything. That's just not what it's about.

Shannon:

I want to know: what type of legacy do you want to leave? What do you want people to say about you at your funeral?

Eric:

That's a tough question.

Money is important. It's important to be able to create a lifestyle for your family. It's important to be able to create what you... Just as you said, a legacy to pass down, but what I hope my children understand and what I hope that they teach their children and they teach their children, is the importance of value. How important it is to be valued by other people. If I had my way at my funeral, I would love everybody to take turns and just give a speech, a couple minutes, about a time I helped them.

Not for me, but for them. Even if it's, "I remember a time that I needed to go to the airport, and Eric stepped up and took me. He was busy that day, and he still dropped what he was doing and took me to the airport." Even if it's something that little versus, "I remember a time that Eric helped me. My car had been repo'd. He helped me get a new one." And up to bigger things.

It doesn't have to be money. We focus so much on money. Again, money is important, but I think the reason that I was able to even create any money was because of value. It's because I learned first that you provide value. You give until it hurts, and then eventually, you just can't outrun the money.

Dave Diehl

Outdoor enthusiast, adrenaline junkie, entrepreneur, speaker and coach—Dave Diehl is a high-energy, ambitious real estate investor.

Starting from humble beginnings, he launched his entrepreneurial career at a young age when he opened his first lemonade stand. This small and seemingly insignificant event catapulted him into entrepreneurship. Long after this experience, during a short year and a half in the medical sales industry, he was directly involved with the sales team to generate a half a million dollars in sales revenue per month.

As a serial entrepreneur he has raised in excess of $1 million in capital for six different startups.

Dave's story goes so much deeper than raising money and investing in startups and real estate. Just 6 years ago, he was involved in a near-fatal automobile accident that changed his perspective on life and its irreplaceable value. Not only does he have a real passion for business, but he also has a love for life that will help inspire anyone he comes in contact with to crush their limitations. He captures this love of life with his beautiful wife of 6 years, who he loves spending as much time as possible with exploring the great outdoors. Dave also has a solid belief in giving back to the community for all of the generous blessings he's received, and he's devoted countless service hours to his neighborhoods and church. One of the main mottos he lives by is to live every day like it's your last.

Contact Info:
Thebigdiehl.com
Mammothproductsllc.com
dave@thebigdiehl.com

Shannon:

What inspired you to get into real estate?

Dave:

To me, real estate is something that's always been attractive. I've been an entrepreneur for the last 15 years and involved in several different industries. However, real estate is where I've always wanted to end up because it's what the wealthy do.

There will never be a time when real estate isn't an essential part of living. The key is learning how to engage effectively in the industry. As long as you stick through the difficult times, adapt to the learning curve, and understand the market, you're bound to have success.

Shannon:

How do you think your education in real estate has changed the way you invest?

Dave:

The biggest thing is that the majority of the guesswork and risk has been removed from the equation. Prior to my real estate investing education, I was learning from Google, YouTube, but also by watching other people make mistakes. For example, when I started my shaved ice business, it was more of a trial and error approach that cost a lot more time and money in the long run. At the beginning, we had great success with special events. When we saw others having success with permanent locations, we decided to pursue that avenue. We found a location in a car wash parking lot and went to work. In order to open for business, we had to get the car wash rezoned, our building inspected by the health department, and an expensive, necessary underground electrical line run for permanent power.

It was a great learning experience, but at the end of the day, we ended up having major construction right in front of us where we were located. This issue had an impact on our sales numbers and projections. My wife and I ended up working the business 10-12 hour days the whole summer because we couldn't afford to pay anybody. We ended up breaking even and decided the return was not worth it in keeping the business.

Transitioning to real estate, I said to my wife, "The next business we start, I want to have as much understanding, knowledge, and education about the industry as possible to eliminate the mistakes we made when we were learning by trial and error." By gaining more knowledge and insight in an industry, you remove a lot of the unknowns moving forward.

Shannon:
When people come to you for advice on how to get started in real estate, what do you recommend that they do first?

Dave:
There are several different types of real estate strategies. Decide which of those you want to pursue, then search out and interview as many experts in that area as you can. The more data you can gather, the more precise your decisions will become. During this interview process, stay focused on your moral compass. There are many professionals doing real estate transactions in an unethical way. Integrity and ethics will be the key to building a successful business and reputation.

Shannon:
Do you have a team or do you do it alone?

Dave:
I prefer to work with a team because the job is executed more professionally and efficiently. Having the right team helps develop a system of operation to streamline the process, so the job is done right the first time. Also, developing trustworthy and ethical relationships, like those on a team, will be one of the most important things to starting any business.

For example, recently, we had a deal go south because we had the wrong team in place. Through that experience we learned many valuable lessons. I have since built a team of contractors, lenders, and real estate agents I can trust to get the job done. There are still hidden variables, but it allows you to more quickly anticipate challenges and have more collaboration, which is key to creating the best end product.

Shannon:

When you do your next "fix and flip," what's the first thing you're going to watch for?

Dave:

Simply put... people. The right people on the team make or break a flip. Unfortunately, that's what killed us on this last property. We thought that we had done our due diligence.

We had 3 contractors give us bids. The first contractor said that it was a complete rebuild. The second said that it was a little more work than he could handle, which we respected. Naturally, we went with the third, who said he could do it all. This was the first time my partner and I had used this contractor, but he came highly recommended from a couple of other people. I know now that if someone says they can "do it all" themselves, it's a major red flag! He had a couple guys that came in and did the job completely wrong, so we ended up bringing in a specialized contractor to assess the situation. After the new contractor looked at the electrical work, we found out it wasn't up to code and was extremely dangerous, so we had to completely redo it. It cost us much more than we had planned in our budget because we had to pay for the job twice. If we would have just hired an electrician the first time, we would have saved money in the long run. The good news is that we now have a great checklist.

Before hiring a new contractor:

1. Make sure they use specialized subcontractors for plumbing, electrical, framing, etc.
2. Inspect their completed projects or properties and have detailed conversations with at least 3 to 5 references.
3. When you speak to any contractor or subcontractor, ask about overall experience, craftsmanship, draw schedule, completion time, honesty, etc. And definitely be specific with your questions. This is gold and will save you a lot of energy, time, and money.

When you have the right team in place and do your homework, it will mitigate many unknowns. Moving forward, I will be asking the right questions, doing my research, and really tightening up my interview process before I add anyone new to my team. As a good friend and mentor once told me, "If you think it's expensive to hire a professional, try hiring an amateur."

Shannon:

What do you think is the best strategy for finding "fix and flips?"

Dave:

There are a lot of different avenues, and I don't know that there's a so-called "best." It depends on many factors. A lot of the properties I've found have been through different agents, whether it's a traditional listing or a pocket listing (a property the agent finds before it hits the MLS).

Another strategy is local classifieds. In Utah, I use KSL and Craigslist. I've been able to find a lot of different properties using both sites. Most of these are "For Sale by Owner," which can potentially allow for more creative negotiations.

Being observant and aware during your day-to-day activities is a great way to find leads as well. My partner came across a house that had a "For Sale by Owner" sign. He ended up calling, and long story short, he negotiated the purchase of the property using a subject-to strategy. This is when you purchase the property using the existing mortgage. It really saved him a lot of time and money. He was able to rehab the property quickly and rent it out for a year. This approach almost immediately created a steady, passive income stream. He's since sold it for a net profit of roughly $80,000. Opportunity truly is available if you have the knowledge to execute. Plus, creative strategies come from being educated and prepared. To sum it up, get educated and get creative.

Shannon:

It sounds to me like you do most of your business in Salt Lake City and surrounding area. Is that right?

Dave:

Yes.

Shannon:

Do you think that, in the future, you'll start doing real estate investing in cities you don't live in?

Dave:

Yes.

Shannon:

But why not now?

Dave:

I would really be doing myself a disservice. There's a lot of opportunity in Salt Lake City right now, and I really want to capitalize on the growth. As I start to understand the industry better and know exactly what to look for, relationships will continue to develop and take me outside of Salt Lake and across the nation. For example, I was talking to another investor a couple of days ago, and he was telling me how great the market is in Illinois and how cheap properties are. You can purchase properties for roughly $20,000 and create cash flow of $400 almost immediately. Those are the kind of opportunities and the kind of relationships that can grow and develop over time.

Shannon:

Do you feel like living in Salt Lake City has given you an advantage because the area has a stronger economy?

Dave:

Yes, definitely. We've got a lot of different tech startups moving in and a lot of growth that's happening, which also makes it more competitive. You've really have to be on your "A game" in that sense and have a bigger team out there, so you can find the better deals. A lot of people will tell you, "It's such a tough market out there. There are no deals to be had." That's true—it is tough market because there are a lot people investing in real estate, but the reality is, there's always a deal to be had. Sometimes, there might even be a deal right around the corner that nobody knows about because they haven't asked the right question to the right person to make the deal happen. That's why we have to stay alert at all times. Another tip: listen to the people around you. Some people would call that "eavesdropping." I prefer to call it "resourceful."

Shannon:

What's the first question to ask someone if you're walking down the street, and you see a "For Sale by Owner" sign?

Dave:

"Why are you selling your home?" That's the first question I ask. Based on the response, you can continue the conversation and take it a few different ways. Find out what's motivating them to sell. Are they on a time constraint? Are they behind on payments? Do they own the home free and clear? Are they open to creative financing? Are they looking to make a quick profit? People can be funny until they're asked the right question. If they're in any sort of tough situation, they may not be very open or trusting. Especially if they haven't heard about certain investment scenarios available to them.

Shannon:

Let's say you're getting into real estate and you're starting with little money or bad credit, what are some strategies to get started if you don't have any seed money?

Dave:

The answer to that would be OPM... or what's better known as "other people's money." Many people are always looking for different investments, especially right now. I talk to people who are in their mid-to-late 50's, and they're constantly complaining about how bad their retirement accounts are doing. When I come to them and say, "How would you like to lend with me on my next deal if I could double or triple your rate of return backed by real estate?" It provides a solution people often don't know about. As real estate investors and entrepreneurs, we're problem solvers. When you solve a problem for someone else, you've created a solution that becomes a win-win scenario for both parties. Everybody's happy and excited!

Shannon:

Have you come to a situation yet where somebody lends with you on a deal and then they decide that they want to become a real estate investor rather than just letting you use their money?

Dave:

In that type of scenario, it actually works out pretty well. If they want to get into real estate and actually invest, it doesn't mean that they're not open to a joint venture/partner agreement on a deal where they can introduce you to their circle of influence. Hypothetically, when you create a good experience, people go, "Hey, this is pretty cool." They start referring their golf buddies, friends, or family.

Then you have a referral aspect that begins to develop and benefit you in the long run. Again, at the end of the day, you're just trying to create that win-win solution and solve people's problems. If they want to get into real estate, then you've solved their problem.

Shannon:

What advice would you give to someone who's allowing fear to hold them back from starting their real estate investing?

Dave:

This question is great because we all have fears. Why do some of us have more than others?

There are 2 ways to look at fear:

1. It could be false expectations that appear as if they're a real danger.
2. Or it could be that we simply need to face everything and rise up.

What is fear? Fear itself isn't real. It's a made up concept that's deep within our minds. Fear is a thought that hits you and says, "No, you can't do this; this is too hard." Or it can say something like, "you're not good enough to do this."

We all have the skillset, ability, and the talents to move through fear and accomplish whatever dream or goal we have. The best piece of advice I can give would be to really start to develop yourself. Understand who you are as a person and what you're capable of.

Once you do, believe it.

Read books, listen to different audio books, listen to speakers and trainers, etc. Any way that you can, get the content that's readily available to help you become better. It's just a decision away.

The only differences between the unsuccessful and the ultra-successful is that the ultra-successful have overcome the fear to make decisions and take massive action.

Shannon:

How do you define success?

Dave:

I would define success as fulfilling my potential as a human being. We each have talents and skills that other people don't. We have to develop those skills and develop those talents. Success isn't defined by money or by material possessions. It's defined by achieving your full potential as a human being and helping other people to do the same. If you do that, you unconsciously develop all aspects of life you're trying to create. Life is about being happy. If we can become unbelievably happy and excited about life, the journey to success occurs naturally. That's when the opportunity to influence and help others becomes a reality.

Shannon:

Do you have a favorite inspirational or business-related book?

Dave:

Think and Grow Rich by Napoleon Hill is one of the best books ever written. I absolutely loved that book. I am currently reading *The Inner Game of Tennis* by Timothy Gallwey. It's about a tennis coach that talks about tennis as a mindset. Tennis isn't necessarily the skill or the concept, but it's the mindset you're in. Basically, the way he breaks it down is that you have 2 selves, Self-One and Self-Two. Self-One is the one who's saying, "Oh, you idiot. Why did you hit the ball like that? You're a moron. What are you doing?"

Self-Two is more of the muscle memory and action that's involved with learning and engaging through doing. It goes back to that mindset theory that the only reason you don't do something or you cannot do something is because you tell yourself that you can't do it. I really like that book because of this idea. It's interesting to me that we all have a "Self-One." Most of us would never talk to other people as poorly as we talk to ourselves. We would never call anyone else a moron. Why do we do it to ourselves?

I think because we've given ourselves approval to. I listened to this other book that was also really good. It's called Zero Resistance Selling. Maxwell Maltz gave the example of this little boy who was in a school play. When he went to perform his part, he got really nervous and ended up wetting his pants. After his Dad wouldn't talk to him for a week, the kid felt miserable, and the girls all made fun of him. Now he's in a sales career 35 years later, afraid to talk on the phone and afraid to talk to women because of this experience that happened so long ago.

We give ourselves approval to talk bad to ourselves because of the different things that have happened in our lives. One of the habits successful people have learned how to break is negative self-talk. They've learned how to develop a positive mental attitude along with positive self-talk. For example: "You can do it. You're taking the right steps. Keep pushing and you've got this."

A third book I feel is inspirational is The Traveler's Gift by Andy Andrews. It tells the story of a character who is going through some really tough times in his life, and the journey of change that happened through the different experiences he had. Eventually, he sees himself at the end of this troublesome road, accomplishing his goals and dreams. He was able to reflect on how much he influenced people and the city he lived in.

What you have to realize is... life's about giving back to other people. The more you give, the more you'll receive. It's an inevitable concept called "The Law of Reciprocity". When you give to other people, you help them achieve their goals and dreams, then you automatically reach your own goals and dreams. By developing yourself, you'll find the success and happiness you desire. And when it comes down to it, there are so many good books out there! I challenge everyone to go find them and share what you learn with the world.

Shannon:

Who is your favorite trainer or speaker?

Dave:

I love Les Brown, Jim Rohn, Eric Thomas, and Darren Hardy. Woody Woodward has also been an especially huge influence. I was introduced to Woody about a year and a half ago, and I love his concepts with the Emotional Fingerprint. Basically, people have a message to share, and that message can influence and help you if you're open to it. A lot of people give me grief for always listening to or reading motivational content. They'll say something like, "Oh, you're listening to your motivational stuff again." I'm like, "Heck yeah, I'm listening to this stuff again. What are you doing? You're listening to the radio, or NPR, or this stuff that doesn't help you develop as a person. I'm going to develop to become the best that I can, so I can be a world influencer and game changer." I don't understand why everyone doesn't want to do that? I guess it's good because we need leaders and we need followers. I choose to lead.

Shannon:

What is your definition of the word "success?"

Dave:

It's interesting that you ask. When I sat down with a good friend and mentor of mine, I asked him the same question: "What's your definition of success?" He said, "The biggest thing for me is gratitude and a positive mental attitude." That's the key right there; a positive mental attitude becomes a game changer. I'm reminded of a quote, "You cannot lift another soul until you're standing on higher ground than he is. You cannot light a fire in another soul unless it is burning in your own soul."—Harold B. Lee. In order to help another, you have to get to the higher ground first.

Shannon:

Some of us know what we want to do, some of us don't, and some of us figure it out as we go. Some of us even change daily, but we're all right here, right now. Yet, when you think about the future, what type of legacy do you want to leave behind?

Dave:

I feel most accomplished when I think big. I'm a world changer and innovator. We all have an opportunity to give back to the world, and I feel most accomplished when I have the opportunity to help someone in need. I don't need the credit or the approval. None of that's important to me. What's important is to help people understand that they have the ability to make decisions and choices to take action.

I'm currently working on some of my life's work right now, particularly a book called The Power of Decision and Influence of Choice. For me, I want to leave behind a legacy that helps people understand that they always have a choice. You don't have to go with the status quo or be influenced by the opinions of others. You have the power to make that one choice, that one decision, that will influence more people than you could have ever imagined.

It goes back to the ripple effect. You throw a stone in the water and as soon as that stone hits, what does it do? It doesn't just make one ripple; that ripple continues to grow and creates more ripples until, eventually, it spreads across the whole space that water's contained in. That's what I see happening. I want to give people the okay to say, "You know what? I do have a choice; I can make a decision. I'm not governed by the opinions of others. As soon as I take that action step, I'm out of my comfort zone, and I'm doing more than I ever would have prior to someone else's influence." The final piece of advice I would leave everyone with is to be progression oriented. Always go the second mile and live with integrity, because at the end of the day that is the purpose of life.

Richard & Jennifer Galarse-Pancoast

Jennifer Galarse-Pancoast graduated in 2004 from Seattle University with a Bachelor of Science Degree in Nursing and Minors in Biology and Psychology and started working as a Registered Nurse at The Queen's Medical Center in 2005. Richard Galarse-Pancoast earned an Associate's Degree in Information Systems at University of Phoenix in 2008, which he utilized in jobs at Best Buy's Geek Squad and at the local cable company as a playback air technician.

In 2013, Jennifer and Richard became clients of Sweep Strategies, a Hawaii based financial education company. Through the education and coaching from the staff of Sweep Strategies, the couple was able to reach their financial goals in an accelerated manner by obliterating credit card and student loan debt, in addition to saving large sums of money on home mortgage interest. After seeing what Sweep Strategies taught, Richie decided he would better benefit his family by becoming an instructor for the company and so, he left the IT field.

Seeing how these strategies increased their cash flow, the couple decided to become real estate investors. Now, they're both incredibly passionate about sharing with others how almost anyone can do the same to achieve financial independence.

Contact Info: galarseinc@gmail.com

Shannon:

What inspired you both to get into real estate?

Richie:

Well, the first thing that hit me when I saw a real estate investor doing really well, he was only around 40 years old. I was working at Best Buy's Geek Squad at the time, selling and installing home theater systems for really wealthy people. I had a picture of this client's house, which was overlooking beautiful Makaha Valley on the west side of Oahu, Hawaii. Being able to see that from your home, just this beautiful view, it really blew me away.

While I was installing this gentleman's home theater system, I was wondering what he did for a living, because he looked so young. When he told me he was retired, I didn't understand what he actually meant. Back then, I thought that a retiree was somebody putting money aside in a bucket, like a retirement account, and being able to draw from it when they stopped working. What he told me was that he was in real estate investing. Being somewhere around 40 years old and having great success in real estate investing— it showed me a path, something more than just what I was doing at Best Buy where you just turn in the hours for the money we make.

That experience gave me the ability to share this with my wife. My newfound perspective of seeing beyond what we were doing at the time was eye opening. I'm guessing that really helped her see something beyond "hours for money." What do you think?

Jennifer:

When he shared with me what he saw at his job site that day and talking to this gentleman who was able to retire from working a job at such a young age, it opened my mind to learning about real estate as well as the idea of becoming an investor. It was something I never really thought about before. From what I understood, you needed a lot of money to become an investor. It took quite some time for me to grasp that it could be done with no money out of our pocket. It was the first realization for me that investing in real estate, specifically using the buy and hold strategy for passive income from rental properties, could be much more fruitful than relying on a job to fill a bucket in an effort to get you where you want to be from a financial aspect in life.

I had been a nurse for about 6 years or so. I'd been putting in grueling 12-hour shifts at the hospital, and that's where I was in my life. I only worked part-time, but because of the nature of the job— it sure felt like I was putting in full-time hours, especially having an infant and a toddler at home to care for when I wasn't working. I thought that way of working was how the rest of my life was going to be, since I was making really good money and able to support my family. We have 2 young children, and I thought that where we were at in life at that time was pretty good because we were doing well enough to be able to support our family.

But the stress of the job really took its toll on me. With the idea of becoming real estate investors... it was then when I allowed myself to see that there could be another way, a better way than having to exchange my time as a nurse for how we were going to support our family and grow. It also meant a way to attain the dreams we wanted for ourselves and for our children.

Shannon:
How can someone with poor credit or that's living paycheck to paycheck get into real estate?

Richie:
We didn't have the greatest credit in the world at the time when we started using this strategy. We felt like, at the time, we'd have to build our credit up and have to do something about it. Let's just say that you weren't in that position; you weren't able to actually build your credit. There are still so many ways to create relationships that will eventually turn into a funding source.

For example, being able to use other people's money in so many ways. Let's say if you have an uncle who has $10,000 sitting in the bank at a savings account of 0.03% which is generally the consensus across all banks it seems right now anyway.

That's not much really. It's not doing anything, and he's probably over there bleeding money in interest on other debt. He just doesn't know that his money is sitting in a savings account earning very little interest and his debt is sitting in a debt account costing him more interest. He doesn't see the effect, and he doesn't see it going on. He doesn't understand the structure. What you can actually do is teach him, "Hey, if you let me use that $10,000," and of course with the relationship contract and everything we would learn in real estate, "To use that $10,000 to create more income for you, would you be interested?"

There's so many ways to use other people's money. We ended up using more of the bank's money than anything because we had okay credit. It wasn't the greatest, again, but we were able to qualify for bank product that would be able to help us pay off the debts that we currently had and increase our cash flow dramatically, because the way it works is that $36,000 of student loan and credit card debt was eating up our cash flow like crazy. When we were able to take care of it in interest reducing, debt accelerated way of dealing with debt, we increased our cash flow immediately by $800 per month through making one slight change in how we banked. Then, from there, it started building because, as we paid down, the cash flow started going up, less money going into interest and more money going towards the principal; therefore, accelerating it.

We started using this strategy because it started building our credit faster than we ever thought possible. We don't promise that it's always going to happen that way, but for us

that's what happened. With that credit building, it gave us the ability to tap into the banks even more so. We had that mortgage that was $2600 a month. Well, we were able to actually use this same strategy to shrink that mortgage payment down to $500 a month.

Now looking at the mortgage, it was split up between PITI plus PMI at $2600. The interest alone was around $2,000 a month. But if we could drop that down to $500 a month, then we were able to free up even more cash flow to be able to wipe out more on the house faster, which then give us equity. The equity of the house gave us the ability to dive deep into the liquid asset we've been putting our money into all this time. We just didn't know that it was in front of our face until we learned about it.

Shannon:

Do you invest in other areas in the nation or is all of your real estate in Hawaii?

Richie:

Well, actually, the only real estate we have in Hawaii is our owner/occupant home! Right now, the market is going insane in Hawaii. Using that money and being able to justify a good return on investment is pretty hard right now.

In our position, we're able to look at other places. We do have a rental in Salt Lake City, Utah. We also have a "fix and flip" going on in Salt Lake City as well because we have an awesome relationship with teams over there, boots on the ground and everything we need.

We also have a private money deal out in Georgia. We're looking into Portland as our next step. In fact, one of the things we've been wanting to do is leave Hawaii and turn this owner/occupant into our rental here. Considering that the rental market over here is quite nice and the way we have our setup on finance, it's going to cash flow really well. In fact, to the point where, wherever we decide to move, we could probably rent out a very nice property or open up a new loan on a new property and have it taken care of by the cash flow this property puts out.

Shannon:

Why on earth would you want to leave Hawaii? Where could you go that would be comparable, so that you guys still have the financial stability, but you also have all of the perks you get in Hawaii?

Jennifer:

We do get that question a lot when we share with others our dream of moving our family up to the mainland. The biggest reason is the quality of life. Many people think of Hawaii as paradise. Sure, we have the beautiful beaches, the ideal weather 99% of the year. As I mentioned earlier, we do have 2 young children, and they're now 6 years old and 8 years old. Our main goal is to move them up, most likely to Oregon. We really like the Pacific Northwest area. There are many more opportunities for them in the mainland, along the lines of education, life experiences, and travel. Like their parents, our little ones really love to travel and explore new places.

Richie:

We have maybe 4, 5 places we could take our kids, and I think they're getting bored of all these places here in Hawaii. We're on an island, and of course, we've got the beaches, but the kids are getting tired of the Bishop Museum or the Waikiki Aquarium, the Honolulu Zoo, this Discovery Centre that they have.

We have this beautiful house on our vision board from Portland, actually from Vancouver, Washington that overlooks over to Portland. Yeah, that's our dream house.

Jennifer:

Another reason that really pushes us to move is just the fact that we're growing our business in real estate investing and so being from Hawaii, the travel costs are very high. For instance, when we want to attend conferences and classes, check out properties, even just networking in the communities where we think of investing, travel costs are a significant item of consideration in order to make those business trips happen. We think that moving would really put us in a better position to be able to expand our real estate investing capabilities.

Shannon:

Are those costs which you have to work into the cost of acquiring a home?

Richie:

Yeah. Absolutely.

I feel that I've met enough real estate investors who are successful at what they do that they can just travel pretty much anywhere they want. Being able to come back home to check on the property, even build more relationships, even start doing real estate here when the market starts to calm down a little bit... that's always open as well. We don't feel like we're going to miss Hawaii or the weather or anything like that because we can just make it happen anytime.

Jennifer:

It'll always be home. Hawaii will always be home. It's definitely our goal to be able to have the leisure as well as the means to come back home anytime for a visit. Being the budding investors and entrepreneurs that we are, an idea we frequently discuss is perhaps buying a property such as a beach house or luxury condo, putting it up on AirBnB for that passive income, so it would be profitable when we personally are not using it, and have the liberty of blocking out the dates for our own use when we plan to visit home.

We just want to focus on business growth and quality of life for our family and well-being for our children.

Shannon:

What led you to do the investments in Salt Lake City? Did you just crunch the numbers right or did you have a good team there?

Richie:

It was a combination of both, actually. It just turns out that for the position we were in at the time, whether it be financially and at the education level that we were at, having a relationship with the team over there, really made it a soft landing when we started over there. It's just been nothing but amazing. We couldn't have asked for a better team to work with, we couldn't have asked for a better property to have, we couldn't have asked for a better property manager.

They've just been doing amazing work over there. Even with whatever issues that may have come up between last October until now with our rental, everything's just been so relaxed. Considering that everything we do with our finance education and tying that into our real estate education, it's become so easy. We go in fearless now. That's the beautiful thing about it. It's when we educate ourselves in real estate and in finance, we can go in fearlessly and partner up with really good people, so they could be fearless with us.

The next property we're working on over there is because of the relationship we've built from the first property. It's a "fix and flip" that's in the process. In fact, we're in contract right now. The commissions on this one are pretty amazing!

Shannon:

When you say that you have a team, are these co-investors or are they people that helped you find the properties or is it a combination of both?

Richie:

It's a combination of both. This first house we invested in was just basically meeting somebody and really hitting it off with them. His name is Landon and another gentleman named Ralph. They both introduced themselves because I, myself, went over there to Utah for a conference. I was teaching some of the finance strategies along with a couple of other instructors.

They wanted to know more, so we sat down, we talked, and then in exchange I said, "Well, I could show you a few things with this, but with that being said, do you guys have any deals? We'd like to look into investing in Salt Lake City because with Hawaii being in the uptick on their market and becoming a little more unaffordable or the return on investment is just dropping as it goes." And they agreed. They said, "Yeah, we have something right now, in fact, where we're looking for a buyer. We're getting a "fix and flip" done right now. It's almost done, and we're looking for a buyer. This might be something you could be interested in."

It just so happened after those multiple conversations, multiple call-backs and negotiations, and learning with each other on how this relationship will go from here on out, we made it such a win-win situation that the relationship is very strong now. We can't wait to keep going on that.

Shannon:

Are they wholesalers?

Richie:

No. Landon is actually a pro at "fix and flips." Ralph is a Realtor and a broker who just so happened to team up with Landon on finding deals for them both work on. As it turns out, when looking at our roles with them, we're buyers and we're funders. This team-up that we have is a trifecta of what we need to keep going.

Shannon:

You guys are this perfect little triangle where you're not all trying to be the same. If you all of a sudden decided that you wanted to be a real estate agent or a broker, it would almost break your wheel?

Richie:

Yeah. Being able to leverage other people's skill sets in this is huge. We know what they're doing. We know exactly how they work, but they do it so well, so let them do it.

With the finance side of it, they trust us for how we can use our finance strategy to make it work for us and make it a win-win for everyone. As it goes along, we're teaching each other. We're educating each other on everything we do. It's a really, really good relationship.

Shannon:

Once you get more rentals on the mainland and get to move closer, will you try and save more money by managing your own properties at that point?

Jennifer:

Actually, it's funny you mention that, because one of my favorite parts of having our rental property in Utah is our property manager. We really don't have any interest in managing our own properties, especially since our rental property is in a state different than where we reside in. When we met our property manager in Utah, I told him I was so grateful for him and his team for all they do in managing the rental; with every issue that has come to light, every problem that came up with our tenant or something going wrong in the home itself, I told him that I have yet to experience a headache because their team does such an excellent job at what they do.

We pay them that money and they earn every penny of it. A lot of people have the opposite opinion that they can create more cash flow if they manage their own property.

Richie:

Because of what we know on how to actually leverage our bank product against these properties, it gives us that ability to save even more than what we're paying the property managers. We might as well go that route. We can do both, but to us, I feel like, why not be able to trade it off? Why not be able to keep it a win-win situation and build that relationship with them because they do it so well?

Jennifer:
The way I see it too is that having the property manager is actually an incredible return on investment for us for many reasons, but the most important to us is that peace of mind the property will always be taken care of.

Shannon:
What type of legacy do you want to leave behind?

Richie:
When thinking about our legacy, it really does bring tears to our eyes because we like to look at where we came from. Being able to see where it all started. Here, talk about your dad a little bit.

Jennifer:
When I can compose myself... My late father was an immigrant from the Philippines. He grew up working in the rice fields, and that was all his family ever knew, hard labor out in the hot sun. He had a dream to move to Hawaii because he wanted a better life for himself. He, along with his siblings, found the courage to make that dream come true and settle in Hawaii with plans to seek and create a better life than what he had in the Philippines.

When we talk about leaving a legacy, I look at my dad and remember seeing how hard he worked. After he moved to Hawaii, he met my mother, and they got married, had myself and my sister. They both worked so hard at their jobs (my dad as a laborer for a cement company, and my mom as a certified nursing assistant in a nursing home) to provide for our family and just create a better life-style than each of my parents knew growing up. The biggest lessons I've learned from my dad was the integrity of having a good work ethic and to always put your family first.

When I look back at the legacy he created, what we want to do is give honor to the sacrifices he made in order to put our family where we are today. Learning from my dad's example and having that strong work ethic has really prepared me to see how I could apply that to the next level. That is, my husband and I promoting ourselves from W-2 jobs into entrepreneurship and taking control of how we want to change our family's trajectory of life for generations to come. I look at everything my dad has done, and in order to honor his hard work, I feel like it's my responsibility to show that his choices, his sacrifices, did not go unnoticed, and he really was able to change our family's destiny, so now it's about continuing and building upon that legacy.

Jeff & Janet Grenier

Jeff and Janet Grenier have been entrepreneurs for over 25 years. They have owned many businesses, including brick and mortar, online and work from home companies. They currently own three successful companies and will be expanding to a fourth by the end of 2016. They have enjoyed living a life of financial freedom and helping others get out of the rat race. Their current passion is real estate investing and teaching financial literacy. They are sharing this unique opportunity with as many people as they can in the hopes of creating a better world now and for future generations. Both their sons, Matthew and Jonathan, have chosen to follow in their footsteps and are becoming empowered and successful young men. Jeff and Janet have been happily married for 24 years. They live in Plainfield, Illinois, with their sons and their dog, Wylie. They enjoy spending time with family and friends, meeting new people, going for rides on Jeff's Harley and traveling abroad. They are committed to helping people better their lives, and fulfilling not only their dreams and aspirations but helping others achieve the same.

Conact Info:
idealbizgroup@sbcglobal.net

Shannon:

What inspired you to get into real estate investing?

Jeff:

We were inspired by the person who brought us in, which was Jan's cousin, Mike Pesek. We visited them in Christmas of '14. Mike had a union job that he had been working for twenty-some years. I asked him how it was going, and he said he didn't work there anymore. I asked him why he would give up a pension and all of the other benefits. He explained that he had been networking with a group of real estate investors and liked what he saw. Ironically, we too saw what they did and were inspired to make a change. We knew we could do the same.

Shannon:

Was one of you more inspired to start in real estate investing?

Did one of you say, "Oh my gosh, yes, let's do this!" and it took some convincing for the other person? Or did you both just say, "Yes let's do this!"?

Jeff:

You know what's funny is, we've had many different opportunities over the years, but for some reason this one really stood out. The presenter, Scott Rowe, was explaining what the group had to offer, what it was all about, and the opportunity. In my head, as it's going on, I'm saying to myself, "How do I convince Janet that this is awesome?" They treated the education as though a fourth-grader could do it. All I could think was that it was perfect for us. The funny thing was when the presentation was over, she turned to me and said, "We're doing this!"

Shannon:

Have you always been in business together?

Jeff:

We've been married twenty-four years next month. We do everything together, we're best friends.

Shannon:

Do you think being best friends with your spouse helps in business relationships?

Jeff:

The support system is phenomenal. I've done a lot of different things, and Janet supports me in everything I do. I support her just the same. We don't always necessarily agree that what the other person is doing is the right thing, but we always support each other. We always have each other's back.

Shannon:

Janet, what do you have to add to that?

Janet:

Well, yes, I think when you're having an off day, or vice versa, the other person usually is not, so they can give them support and build them up, "Don't worry about that", or "Stuff happens."

Shannon:

Since you two always have the support of each other do you think that you should still have a one-on-one mentor or group support?

Jeff:

We have both. Not only do we have one-on-one with a specific mentor, we have one-on-one with many mentors. Then we have the groups, as well. The nice thing about the groups, is that questions are asked that you don't even know you have until you hear the question, or that somebody's afraid to ask. Even then, you can go even further after the group, and go one-on-one with a mentor. The nice thing is, we mentor everybody. Everybody helps everybody here. We all work together, and this may sound funny, but in our organization, there's really no competition. We all work together.

Janet:

I'll tell you, when we first went there, it kind of freaked me out, because the world doesn't work that way normally, and all I was thinking was, "Who are all these strange people?" Now that we're a part of it, I've come to love the community. I've also realized that they really aren't strange!

Jeff:
We meet every Thursday night, and we told our mentors, "If you think I'm coming here every Thursday night, you're nuts, it'll never happen." It's been fifteen months, and I have not missed a Thursday yet!

Shannon:
What is the most exciting group meeting you have attended and what is the best idea that you took from it?

Jeff:
Right now, we're in a study group that is based on buy and hold strategies and holding properties. We came into this community not knowing a thing, outside of buying our own house. That's the only real estate knowledge that we had.

Janet:
Right now, we're in the buy and hold group, which is about rental properties. We learned so much about making passive income, creating legacies for our families. Helping people out there, who need properties to live in, because face it, we all need food, and we all need shelter. We know that we can provide shelter for people out there who need it. It's fabulous. We know how to help people who can't afford their mortgage because they've lost their job. We know that we can help them by taking over their payments and saving their credit. It is a really cool feeling!

Shannon:
Why is passive income important to you?

Jeff:
Passive income is important to me because we get to play and get paid. It's nice that you can earn money while you sleep. You can be floating

around in the ocean, still making money, and not having to think "how am I going to pay for this? How am I going to do this?" Passive income is important for me because we can help so many people. We can give our time to help more people because we are not going to be trading hours for dollars. We can spend our time working with people who need to improve themselves, and with passive income you can do that. Like I said, you are not trading hours for dollars, you can use your time as you want and still make money while you are doing other things.

Shannon:
How's that ocean working for you guys, living in Illinois?

Janet:
The ocean isn't so great from here which is just one more great reason that we became involved in real estate investing. I love the thought of passive income because we have two sons and it would be nice to have real estate to pass on to them when that point in time comes.

Shannon:
Do you recommend that you manage the rental properties yourself, or that you hire a property management company?

Jeff:
For many reasons, property management all the way.
1. They know the laws; they keep up-to-date with the laws.
2. Nobody wants that 3:00am phone call on Christmas Eve that a water heater went out. That's what property managers get paid for. They are professionals so let them deal with the tenants, let them do what they are there for. Let them do their thing and we will work with the property managers to make sure they are doing things to our standards. Let them deal with the day-to-day dealings with tenants and properties, and all the other stuff.

Shannon:
Janet, if somebody came to you that wanted to get involved in real estate investing and they had very little money, or poor credit, what are some

strategies that they could use so they could actually get into real estate investing?

Janet:
There's always 401Ks that you can borrow money against. There's also whole life insurance. There's also crowd-sourcing you can use. There's a myriad of different ways that people can get funding.

Jeff:
If somebody is serious about it, we can do it. Like Janet's saying, we can borrow from our 401Ks, we can borrow from our IRAs, we can borrow from other people's IRAs, 401Ks, other people's life insurance.

Shannon:
What do you mean when you say you can borrow from your 401K?

Jeff:
Well, there are really two types of 401K. There's your 401K that you have with your employer right now and there are old 401Ks, which are held with companies that you don't work for anymore and that you never did anything with. That 401K is still sitting with that company.

With a 401K you can actually borrow 50% of your money from the 401K, up to $50K. There is interest on that money, but the nice thing is you're paying yourself back that interest. There's a thing called genuine self-directed 401Ks and IRAs. What that means is you can actually determine where your money goes. Not many companies work with genuine self-direction but there are a few custodians which you can find to help you change your standard IRA into a genuine self-directed IRA.

With your 401K, you were probably given a choice of being aggressive, moderate, or like, no risk at all. If you self-direct your IRA, you can actually use all of your money, you get to determine where it goes. There're a few pieces that you can't get into, collectibles, and stamps, and that. This is how money is made for real estate deals. People self-direct their IRA money or their 401K money. Right now, on your 401K you're making, what, maybe two, three percent? We offer twelve to eighteen percent, and it's backed by real estate.

Shannon:
Do you think that in order to be successful in real estate investing the economy needs to be strong?

Jeff:
No.

Shannon:
Is it riskier to invest in real estate when the economy is weak?

Jeff:
Actually now is the best time to get the best deal on real estate. What a lot of people don't realize is that you make your money on real estate when you buy it. You get paid when you sell, but you make money when you buy it. What I mean by that is say you're interested in a property that needs rehab work and it's worth $300,000 and it needs approximately $100,000 in repairs. You work with the home owner and acquire that property for say $150,000. You have $150,000 in equity in the property at that point.

When the economy is bad, people are hurting and they can't manage their mortgage payments. We have many strategies that we can use to take over that mortgage for them. Like a Subject TO. That is, we take over the property but the mortgage remains in the home-owner's name.

Shannon:
Why would people do that?

Jeff:
Because they don't have another option. They can't afford their mortgage. They can't afford to stay in the house. But if we take the property over by Subject TO and we make their mortgage payments, what happens with their credit? Their credit stays good. As a matter of fact, it sometimes improves because we catch up on their payments and

we keep making the payments while we are rehabbing the house. When we sell the house their mortgage gets paid off. In the bank's eyes, or on their credit score, nobody knows they weren't making the payments. The bank doesn't care where the money comes from... they just want the money for the mortgage payment.

Shannon:
Are fix and flips your end goal?

Jeff:
No, our goal is more buy and holds, because we want the passive income. When you do a fix and flip you get paid nicely, but once you sell the house you're done. You can't get paid on that property anymore. I would rather have somebody paying us rent every month. Look at it this way; we're providing a service; we're putting a roof over somebody's head. For that service, they pay us every month to live in that property. For us, we're helping out, we're doing a good thing. That's why we're into that. It's a win-win situation.

We would love to have a legacy to leave to our grandkids, whenever we have them. I've got time to wait though.

Shannon:
What do you want your legacy to be?

Jeff:
That is a great question. I want it to be that we provided well for our family, and for our community. To know that we were people that were generous and we gave our time. We gave our resources, we helped out, we helped make the world a better place. I think that's what all humanity's thing is, is that we should all leave the place better than we found it, wherever we are. For me, for my legacy, it will be that we always left where we were better than we found it.

Shannon:
Janet, what do you want to add to that?

Janet:

I want to pay it forward. If people were to look back on my life, I don't want them to be like, "Oh, she was wealthy." I mean, wealth is, you make it, you lose it, you make it, you lose it. I would rather have a more sustainable legacy, where one will think, "She really made a stamp on the world."

Shannon:

With your buy and hold strategy, do you plan on having all of your properties in your local community? Or do you plan on investing in other areas?

Janet:

Yes, we definitely plan on other areas. My parents are out in the Phoenix area, so we'd like to have properties out that way. Possibly Florida as my sister's out in Florida. I don't know, Jeff, where else did you want to go?

Jeff:

Here and there, to sound a little selfish for us. There are places that we want to go, and we want to buy rental properties there, and here's why: Say we want to go visit her parents in Arizona, and we have rental properties there. We can take that trip down there to visit our rental property, visit her parents, and write-off the whole trip. You've got to use tax write-offs to your advantage, that's what makes the world go around. So, yes, we are going to go into other areas. Places we would like to vacation, so we can use them as a tax advantage while we're there.

Shannon:

What are your goals for 2016?

Jeff:

By the end of this year, we want to have two rental properties up and running. We plan to have four more in 2017. We are working right now to acquire the first two properties. Then, starting next year, we want to add one property per quarter. We are working on the plans for next year and how we're going to do that. You really have to plan these things ahead of time. Our overall goal is to add one rental property per quarter, every quarter.

How important is it to set those goals, and what would you say to someone who sets those goals, and then struggles to attain them?

Jeff:
Your goals are a road map. You wouldn't drive to Florida without knowing how to get there. So you set up goals, and if you don't reach your goal, it's still a success. Then, just tweak your goal a little bit to make it a little more attainable. Figure out why you didn't reach the goal and then tweak it so you can. Did you need to put a little more time and effort into it? Did you set your goal so high that it was unattainable? Figure out what it was, where you went wrong, and fix it, so you can attain it. You have to set goals first. If you don't set goals, you'll have nowhere to go.

Shannon:
Janet, what does success mean to you?

Janet:
I don't think you can be successful unless you help other people in your journey. To me success isn't really definable, it's more of a journey.

It's ever-evolving, and we are ever-changing, hopefully for the better. That's how I would view success. To grow and help people every day. If you do that, you're a successful person.

Shannon:
What are some creative ways that you use to acquire properties?

Janet:
We talk with everybody, we network all the time. We're using a service to send out letter asking "have you ever thought about selling your property?" It's set up for specific people with a minimum amount of equity in their home. We, of course, have agents that send us a lot of properties. We put out signs that say, "We buy houses."

Shannon:

Why do you think people succeed at real estate?

Jeff:

It's like everything else, there're systems in place. That's what we love about what we do. When talking to people who have been doing this for a long time, we ask them a lot of questions. For example, "What makes this one successful, versus the one where you could've been more successful?" They all tell me the same thing, "When you take the classes, and you listen to these experts, and they tell you, do step A, step B, step C, it always seems to work smooth." It's when they want to do step A, go to step C, and maybe go back to step B, that they have issues. I think for success, if you follow a proven person with a proven method that has been successful, and do what they did ...

Janet:

Duplication.

Jeff:

If you can just duplicate what you see somebody successful doing, you will be successful too. It's when you say, "I think that I can cut this corner," that you get in trouble.

Shannon:

What do you think is the number one mistake an individual makes when buying their first investment property?

Jeff:

Not inspecting the property properly, not hiring the right professionals, for example not hiring the right person to inspect the property, not hiring the right attorney to go through the contract, and to be there at closing for you, not evaluating the property properly, not seeing that there are more issues than you first thought. You have to carefully hire your professionals.

People like to do things to save money. But when you're talking about the money you're spending on a property, you have to lay that money out to get the return the way you want it. You hire these professionals. You hire a good inspector, because they are the ones who are going to crawl through the attic, they're the ones who are going to crawl through the crawl-space. They are going to go through the whole property and know exactly what they are looking for. Talking to the inspector that we know, he knows what requires more attention than other things based on the age of the property.

Hiring the right attorney who knows the contracts. Knowing how to get the funds, and how to get the funds that are affordable, to complete the project. How long the project will honestly take when all is said and done.

Doing your due diligence so you know what to expect before it happens.

Janet:
I believe also that for a first-time investor a major problem they would have is that they're not flexible. They go into a deal with one exit strategy and no other options. Say it's a fix and flip and something shifts and it's no longer a viable fix and flip. They don't realize they can change their fix & flip strategy to a rent-to-own strategy or a lease-option, or one of the other exit strategies. Because they don't have the education, they are lacking the knowledge to make these types of decisions and basically to think on the fly.

Jeff:
Rent the property out.

Shannon:
When you are doing your due diligence, and you're crunching the numbers on a home before you purchase it, do you work in all of your utility costs as well?

Jeff:
Absolutely. Yes, all your holding costs like that, your taxes, insurance, all your utilities, all those costs are worked into how long you think you can hold the property. There are formulas they teach you for these

calculations, which is nice. If it's a three-month rehab, you better have six months' worth of holding, because you've got to have the house on the market for three months. What's nice is you can figure out, on average, how many days it takes to sell a house in the area. If you're going into a property where the average days on market is 180 days, that's six months it's on the market. Be prepared to have your repair time plus those six months.

Aaron Hammill

Aaron Hammill majored in Civil Engineering at The University of Texas in Arlington, Texas. As a dedicated sales professional in the steel Industry, he has developed astute consulting and closing skills, building a reputation of persistently increasing revenues each year valued in the multi-million-dollar range. He has since taken these prolific negotiation skills and business acumen into the real estate investment realm.

Passionate about building his investment team and helping others to do the same, Aaron has started his own real estate investment business, The Hammill Group, Inc. (www.hgflats.com), with a mantra of 'Inspire – Educate – Real Estate.' Aaron's mission is to empower others to develop their selves, their education, and their investments, teaming together with like-minded individuals seeking one objective: becoming financially free through self-betterment.

Contact Info:
Aaron E Hammill
info@hgflats.com
www.hgflats.com

What inspired you to get into real estate?

Aaron:
When I was around eighteen-years old, I would wander through Barnes and Noble book store. I always started in the success section, then I would look at homebuilding and trade books. I have always been good with my hands, and I knew that I could have more. I knew that the house on the cover could be my house. I felt different about life. I was not content. I knew that I wanted to be an entrepreneur and go into business for myself so I could have it all.

One day, a book caught my eye. On the front cover it said, "What the rich teach their children that the poor do not." I knew that I needed to read it. I wanted the information that rich people taught their kids. *Rich Dad, Poor Dad*, by Robert Kiyosaki, has inspired so many people in the world, and I was no different. That book made me realize there were other people in the world who didn't want the "expected" life: go to college, get a job, work hard, and retire. Always working for someone else and worried about losing your job because of situations beyond your control. For me, it was reading "Rich Dad, Poor Dad" that made me realize that being an entrepreneur was okay and that investing in real estate was a great way of doing it.

I didn't know how to invest in real estate at eighteen, but it gave me power knowing that others felt the same way as I did, and I took it from there. It gave me that first feeling of acceptance, of feeling like I belonged. I created a couple of small businesses; buying and selling cars was one of those. I was good at working with cars, so it made sense to me. I did not go directly into real estate. I always knew in the back of my head that real estate was the end goal. That was the good life.

Four years ago I started really reading, learning, and networking. I met people that were taking control and intentionally living their lives through real estate investing. Those people, that I now call friends, are truly the biggest inspiration I've had.

Shannon:
At such a young age, did you have a partner in your first business venture?

Aaron:
I did not. I went out on my own. In fact, I tried doing a couple of businesses of my own. I learned the hard way that going into business alone was difficult, and I was not as successful right away as I thought I would be. I actually went into a pretty dark place for a few years. I had failed a couple times, and, really, I wound up homeless. After those few years I woke up and realized that I had to change something. I gave up on the entrepreneurial side of things, temporarily, and went back to school.

I knew that going back to school would be a stepping stone to eventually getting back into business for myself. I realized the way I was trying to do things wasn't working for me, so I would go back and do it the traditional route. I completed college and received my degree in civil engineering.

Now, I'm in sales for a steel producer; I sell steel for skyscrapers here in Chicago and around the US. The traditional route ended up providing me the capital and the confidence to jump out on my own. That's what has gotten me here today with real estate.

Shannon:
What is the best piece of advice that you would give someone who was allowing fear to hold them back from starting their real estate investing?

Aaron:
My advice would be to really evaluate yourself and your situation: make sure that you have a support system around you, that you are learning the correct way to go about whatever interest you're into—whether it be real estate or a tech company or your own lawn mowing company—to have the mentorship and the knowledge to help you get out there because that first year or two is going to be the hardest. If you don't have that mentorship it can be a lot tougher road. I would say evaluate yourself, make sure that you're learning the proper way to do things, and find a couple of mentors to help you along the way.

Shannon:

What do you think is one of the best qualities for a mentor to have?

Aaron:

A good mentor needs to have compassion and love for the person that they're mentoring. That goes further than anything else they can offer. In my situation, he understood that's what I needed because everybody needs different things at different times. If a good mentor can realize what that person needs at that time, they can really help them through anything.

A lot of mentors and coaches will claim that they focus only on specific areas, but really when you dig down deep into someone's issues that they're looking for help with, or trying to get some advice on, you can dig down into deeper layers that weren't really the reason why you asked for help to begin with. It's probably more worth talking about and working on than the issues that you thought you came to that mentor for. Having the awareness of a mentor, and then that compassion and love to give whoever it is that they're mentoring exactly that, helped me the most.

My mentor comes off as kind of a stickler. He has the approach that he's going to really beat you up, motivate you, get you out there, keeping you accountable to take care of your daily tasks that you say you're going to. I was afraid. I had a meeting with him, and I hadn't done the things that I needed to do that we had talked about and that he was going to keep me accountable for. I really thought he was going to lay into me and tell me how a parental figure would, that I needed to shape up or ship out. It wasn't that exactly, but it helped me more than anything. He showed me understanding and compassion about how he knows it can be hard as well and gave me examples of how it was hard for him that week also to get things going. Knowing that someone else there understands and can show you that compassion and love is sometimes all that we all need.

Shannon:

Do you feel that real estate investing success is dependent on a strong economy?

Aaron:

No, not at all. Most investors that you run into will say that they would prefer a weak economy so that they can capitalize on the low cost real estate and the abundance of available real estate out there in an economy that's weak. There's money to be made in a good economy. I think that there is probably a little bit more money and opportunity to be had in a bad economy, at least for real estate.

Shannon:

If you're investing in real estate in a good economy, what should you do differently?

Aaron:

You have to set yourself above the rest. Find a niche and take a good share of that market. Whatever area of the US or real estate investment strategies that you're in, if you can find and carve out a little niche that sets you apart, you can be wildly successful.

I have found here in Chicago that if you buy a large property in a popular neighborhood, set up the inside of the house as a nice livable place with common areas furnished, and then rent each room separately, you can make a significant cash flow. I've rented out these houses room by room demanding significantly higher rents on properties than what most investors would get. These are houses that other investors will back away from in these neighborhoods. They say, "that's not a good investment because you can't get enough cash flow off of it," but they're looking at renting the whole place to one family.

I've found a niche to buy these homes, rent out room by room, make it a nice living situation inside the home, find people within Chicago that are either new to Chicago or are just wanting to find other people to share a home with, get to know new friends, experience the city together, and provide that all to these people, and they're more willing to pay for that experience. If you can find a little niche in any given market, and mine is not an easy market to participate in, there's still a lot of money to be made. You just put your mind to it and get out there, and start really looking at the different situations and what people are looking for.

Shannon:

Do you find that since there aren't as many investors in that niche that you can just own it and do it great?

Aaron:

Oh yeah, definitely. Yep, a big positive to grow the market. It works simply because you have a bunch of thirty-something professionals that are not married, have no children, and want to rent a one-bedroom apartment in a decent area; you're looking at $1800 a month plus all of your expenses. There are several people that will rent rooms instead. You end up having three or four like-minded people living together in a much nicer home, and they're paying $900 to $1500 for a room versus $1800 for an apartment they're alone in all the time. I've jumped on the opportunity and it has been wildly successful. The trick is to always stay ahead of the curve.

Shannon:

As an investor, when you are looking at a property, how do you figure out if there's going to be enough cash flow in that property to make it a wise investment?

Aaron:

I've just run the numbers enough to where I find the following:

The purchase cost.

I add in the cost to renovate the property.

I add in the cost to furnish the property. (If furnishing the entire property with the exception of the bedrooms.)

Then you basically run your numbers as a net-operating income, as you would learn through real estate books on running your numbers

After that, net income is subtracted from your total cash that you're bringing in through rent.

That left over money is basically your cash flow.

On a property that's as expensive as they are here in Chicago, I look to have a decent return in cash flow. On some of these properties here in Chicago it could be from $1500 - $2500 a month cash flow. For me, that's a good number. Really when it comes down to it, it's just learning all the terms in real estate and how to run your own numbers and really knowing what niche it is that you're going after to know those numbers as well. Of course, cash flow isn't your only income in rental properties. Debt pay down and hopefully if you're lucky enough, appreciation in value. Calculating these factors can give you a return on your initial investment, which I have been realizing 50% return on my initial investment money.

Shannon:

Are there any extra costs to be aware of when you are putting together a "rooms for rent" home?

Aaron:

It's really more than just "renting a room." I am really putting together an experience for others. A lot of my extra costs are going to be decorating the place, making sure that it looks nice, with nicer furniture than a lot of places would have. In one house I put an in-home mini theater. I've also thought about adding in maybe a shuffleboard table, or things like that, to make it somewhere that when people view it as a place to live, they know it's a fun place to have gatherings and get to know others. I am selling an experience for people that are new to the city or people that want to make friends and experience the city together. Having a house that's inviting and has those extra things for people to do is a big selling feature.

Of course, you also have to figure in vacancy rates. When people move out you have to consider what kind of vacancy rate you're going to have. Is it going to be one month per house per room that you won't be receiving rent? Each place is going to be unique on its own, but those are two of my main expenses.

If two of the three bedrooms in a house cover the mortgage, then you really have a safe zone. The third bedroom is your cash flow. This helps to make sure that you are protected, even if you have a one or two month vacancy.

Shannon:

Okay, so do you at this point do an all-inclusive type rent? Meaning, are their internet, water, and cable all included in your rent price?

Aaron:

Yes, it is. That's another added benefit into moving into a home like this, not having to worry about those small details. A lot of times when people get together and move into a house they're always worried about splitting the electricity bill, and then you've got to do it to the gas bill, and the cable bill, and the water, and you have to sit down every month and split it out. Then, of course those bills are fluctuating all the time as well, so that adds a little bit of added stress to each person: 'this person likes it warmer or colder, but now I have to pay an extra because they like it like this' sort of thing.

Instead of dealing with all of that, I just do an average of what the utility costs are in each building and then split that between the different rooms and make it a flat rate. Sometimes it will be a little bit more, sometimes it will be a little bit less, but in the end overall it tends to work out, and they just have to worry about paying that flat rate every month; they don't have to worry about are they using the electricity too much or too little and that sort of thing. They can just live their lives, go on about it, and not have stress between each roommate of what's going on with who likes what and pay their flat rate, and that's it.

The great thing about this business model is that it translates to several other areas. I can duplicate this with corporations that are looking for executive housing. I can also market to the traveling nurses. There's a lot of nurses out there that use the program that hospitals will offer, which is basically three-month contracts in all these different cities. In Chicago, Chicago Healthcare is a huge industry here, so a lot of traveling nurses find it's not easy for them to find leasing on places for three months. These traveling nurses don't have that benefit, and they're out there trying to find their own. The trick is finding housing close to the hospital. Location is everything.

Shannon:

Do you manage these properties, or do you have an outside management group?

Aaron:

Currently I manage them, but for the next two that we add on I will be looking for someone else to manage it for me. Everyone has their views on managing or not managing. For me, it's completely worth it to find a property manager and have them take care of those things, so that you can better use your time to go out there and build your business rather than spend it listening, or making calls, to different issues that are going on in the house. There's more than just toilet repairs, though most people use that example. There's so many other issues that arise. If you can find someone, a good property manager, to take care of those things, you can then go spend your time finding that next good deal to help build your business and bring more money to the bottom line.

Shannon:
When you are looking for an investor, where do you look?

Aaron:

Networking. The number one thing when looking for someone to invest in you is trust. They must be able to trust that you know what you're talking about, know what you're doing in any given invest-ment, and have the support around you and the character to do the right thing with their money. You cannot show these characteris-tics to potential investors without networking and showing them in person, repeatedly, over a given period of time. I like to network as much as I can at local real estate groups. Once investors get to know you well enough and are comfortable with you, the money will come. If it does not, then you need to reevaluate what you're doing.

Shannon:
What are two things that you want people to remember about you?

Aaron:

I want people to say that I am inspirational and compassionate. Those are both attributes that I aim for every day.

Dave Jaquish

When I graduated from college, I went to work for Corporate America. That was an eye-opener for me. It was either 'their way or the highway.' I believed there was a better way. So I became a PGA golf professional and managed golf courses for 15 years. It was a decent environment, except I was building someone else's dream and working a lot of hours, including weekends. I was following all the 'rules' of getting ahead—higher education, retirement plan, etc. In 2001, I lost 1/3 of my retirement plan to the stock market. I learned very quickly that I needed to rely on myself and no one else for my financial freedom.

So, I bought a landscaping business in 2003. Business ownership changed my life. I learned to leverage other people's time and efforts to create the life I deserved.

In 2007, I became educated in real estate investing. Then I moved to Phoenix from Wisconsin in 2011. To this day, I continue to use my real estate investment knowledge and the concept of leverage to flip properties in the Phoenix area as well as across the country. I love being my own boss. I am in control of my financial future, and the sky is the limit.

Contact Info:
azjaquish@gmail.com

Shannon:
What inspired you to get into real estate?

David:
In 2007 I sold my landscaping business and knew I wanted to do something different. I had seen some of my friends making money in real estate. They made it look easy. I didn't think it was that difficult of an industry to get into and be successful, but I didn't know anything about it.

So, I asked my friends where they obtained their knowledge, and they said, "Well, we got educated. We didn't know anything about it either until somebody taught us how to do this." I looked into some of the properties they had invested in, and they were making $20,000 to $80,000 flipping houses." I knew that I didn't have the knowledge to create my own real estate investment business yet, but I could follow directions!

Shannon:
Do you think it is important to have friends and mentors in the business in order to be successful?

David:
Yes. My friends were the ones that actually pushed me to get educated in the business. By taking the classes from the professionals that were actually doing the real estate deals now, I started to learn how to invest in real estate. The nice thing was, I wasn't in it all by myself. I surrounded myself with knowledgeable people in the industry that could teach me and mentor me. I would not have been as successful if I had been The Lone Ranger in real estate investing.

Shannon:
What is one of the top real estate strategies that you learned when you were getting this education and why do you like it?

David:
The most important strategy was how to flip houses. Which is where you purchase a property that needs some TLC, fix up the property,

add value to it, and sell it for a profit. This strategy was important because there are tons of opportunity in this market. There's a lot of properties out there that just need to be updated and just as many people looking for a house that they can just unpack the boxes and move in to. They don't want to do the fixing, either because they don't know how to do the fixing and they would rather pay somebody else to do it or because they don't want the hassle.

In fact, we're doing one right now in Sun City. It is a 30-year old house, and there really isn't anything wrong with it. It just needs general updating on the inside, and the pool needs a little work on the outside. It just needs to be dressed up a little bit.

Shannon:

What are the main things that you look out for when you are acquiring a house to flip?

David:

One of the main things to avoid are structural issues because they can get really expensive. I have found that if the house has cracked slabs, cracked foundation walls, or something like that it can eat into your profit margin very quickly. So I won't touch them because the risk is too great. Everything's based on the numbers. You want to have a house that has good bones, that only needs cosmetic things. For example, if it only needs carpet or new flooring, that is a relatively inexpensive fix that really adds value and can increase the house's appeal for very little time and money. Another area that can be easy and inexpensive to update is the kitchen. Sometimes you can dress up a kitchen just by putting in new counter tops. You don't have to change the cabinets necessarily, sometimes a fresh coat of paint or new hardware is all they need to be updated. Again, a lot of these decisions depend on the numbers. Can you make the profit you're looking for? I find a lot of times when you're looking at structural issues, it just gets cost prohibited.

Shannon:

So, then if a house has a structural issue does it make or break the deal?

David:

If the numbers are there, I do the deal. Numbers are numbers. They don't lie. The downside is that sometimes the person that owns the property might think it is worth more than it really is because they may not really understand the significance and how expensive it can be to fix some of these structural issues.

Shannon:

Does the person who owns the property dictate whether you're going to flip the house?

David:

Generally, not. One of the things that I do with house flips is have all my costs together. I'll have bids from contractors with the entire list of things that need to be fixed so the home can be sold at fair market value. When I can show the seller how much it's going to cost to do the repairs and updates that are needed, and share my expertise with them, then they know that I'm not just trying to low ball them. I can show them that there is actually quite a bit of work that needs to be done to resell. I really want them to be aware of what it's going to cost to fix the house. I see a lot of sellers' underestimate what it's going to take.

Shannon:

What are some of the strategies that people with little money or poor credit can use to get started in real estate investing?

David:

I thought when I got started it was going to be difficult for me to invest in real estate because I didn't have a whole lot of money at the time. Once I got educated and realized that I didn't need, "my money," but I needed, "somebody's money," it really opened up doors for me.

We've got private money lenders, and we've got hard money lenders. Once I understood how to ask the right questions of people my strategies changed. A lot of people have money sitting in CD's and retirement plans and a lot of different places. They're looking for a better interest rate or a more secure investment.

If I can talk to them and share some of the things that we do and they can take the retirement plan and invest it in a piece of property, and it's secured by the property, a lot of people like that comfort level. Because in general, that money is not secured when it's in stocks and bonds and mutual funds. It can go up and down and sideways. Mutual fund can go to zero, or a stock can go to zero, but a piece of real estate won't go to zero. Even if it burns down, you still have land to sell that has value.

When I explain that to people, they understand what I'm talking about. This isn't taught in our traditional school system. High school and colleges don't really teach about how to invest in real estate. They teach people how to get a job. As we've seen in the last 6-8 years, that doesn't work really well for a lot of people. Their job can go away through no fault of their own and now what are they going to do?

I owned a landscaping company for four years from 2003 to 2007. Prior to that, I was a W2 employee. I graduated college and was a sales rep for Oscar Mayer for 5 years. I got into Corporate America because that's what my parents did. My dad was in Corporate America for 37 years. I thought that's what you do. You work for the same company for 30+ years and you get a pension plan, a retirement plan; you get all this kind of stuff. When he retired after 37 years I asked him, "You know, how's retirement?" He put his face about two inches from my face, and he said, "If I could have left those people 30 years ago and done something else I would have."

I thought, "How sad." I'm starting to go down this same Corporate America path. I thought, "What can I do to start to generate income on my own, independent of a huge corporation like that?" I became a PGA Golf Professional and started to manage golf courses in the Midwest, mostly in Wisconsin and Illinois. That was an improvement, but I was still working for somebody else. The last job I had, I was managing a golf course in Madison, Wisconsin and it was a family owned golf course. My boss had to hire his brother because his mom said, "Your brother needs a job." He never worked a day in his life in the golf business, but he had the right DNA and I didn't. I wasn't upset with that because I knew I wasn't part of the family and I wasn't going to take over this golf course. I was also the human resources manager and payroll manager, and when I saw his paycheck was twice as much as mine I said, "This isn't going to work." I sat down with the family and I said, "This just isn't fair. You're not going to take advantage of me like this."

I was determined right then and there to find my own way, somehow. That's when I bought my landscaping business. I became my own boss, and that was 13 years ago. I'm so grateful that I don't have to rely on somebody else for my income. That's why I started out with that business, kept it for four years and then, transitioned to a full-time real estate investor. I jokingly tell people I'm the best boss I've ever had. I take vacations when I want. I still work hard, but I can also play hard and not pass the time off. Not wait for my annual review to get a 50 cent an hour raise or $1500 a year bonus. If I want to generate more income I do more real estate deals.

Shannon:
When you discovered that you didn't want to follow the "standard plan" for life what did you do?

David:
When I started my landscaping business I was taking a shot in the dark. I didn't know what I was doing. I mean, I didn't know that many people that were business owners that could mentor me along the way. What I did have business owners tell me was, you will never regret being a business owner. You'll be surprised how freed up your life becomes.

I didn't really believe or understand that. They said, "You're going to work harder for yourself than you will for your employer, but it's going to be much more rewarding." I didn't understand that until I actually got my feet wet as a business owner and realized that they were right. You work very hard, but it's very rewarding. What's more rewarding is when you can start to build your business as opposed to building somebody else's business. You've got something that you've created that has value that's bringing something to the community, that's doing all the things that businesses have the ability to do, and you're not working for a paycheck anymore. You're not trading your time for dollars anymore. You're actually creating your own legacy.

Shannon:

You are originally from Wisconsin, now you're in Arizona, do you find yourself doing more real estate investing in your local area or do you do real estate investing all over the nation?

David:

I do most of my investing right now in Arizona. I love it out here. There is so much opportunity for everything. When I was in Wisconsin, the county I lived in had 35,000 people, which is a pretty small community. If I wanted to do more projects, I'd have to drive about an hour away to get some of this done. I live in Maricopa County now and we've got over 4.5 million people here. There are deals all over the place. I don't have to travel very far to find a deal that has good numbers. I love it here. I also don't have to shovel snow. Which I really like.

Shannon:

Do you feel like success in real estate investing is dependent on a strong economy?

David:

Absolutely not, because I've made money when the economy was going down, and then when the economy came back up. What helps is understanding the economy. It doesn't have to be strong. I am partnered up with somebody right now on a house flip and he says the same thing. He said, "I've made money when the economy goes down, and I've made money when the economy goes up because we got educated and really understand what's important." The thing is, if you've got a cash flowing property by renting it out and the value of the property goes down in the short term, that's not going to affect your cash flow because you are charging a fixed rent and your mortgage payment is fixed as well. If the home value dips during a recession your cash flow from your rents are not affected.

One of the things that I realized in 2008, 2009 when housing prices were going down, rental rates didn't go down, or if they did, they went down very little. If you've got some properties to rent your cash flow is going to stay pretty consistent whether the value of the property goes up or down. I think that's very important for people to understand.

Shannon:

Do you have a favorite investment strategy?

David:

I really enjoy flipping houses the most because I get to see the transformation from kind of a junky house or just a dated house, into something that looks really nice when you are finished. There's satisfaction in turning an eyesore into something that a buyer can be proud to bring their friends to, can move in and unpack boxes and be ready to go. I get a lot of joy out of doing it. We get so many compliments on the properties we've done over the years from buyers coming in and say, "Geez this looks nice. Oh, I like the way this looks. Oh, I'm glad you did that. Oh, you've got granite counter tops, etc." It's just a good feeling to have when you can say I just turned a sow's ear into a silk purse.

Shannon:

What advice would you give someone who is allowing fear to hold them back from starting their real estate investing?

David:

People are fearful about a lot of things. Not just real estate investing, but anything that's new that they don't know anything about. I want people to look back at other things they feared in their life and really see if those fears ever became reality. I would imagine 95% of those fears never happened. The same thing is going to happen in real estate investing. We could be fearful about a lot of things we know very little about and one of the things that reduced my fear was getting the knowledge and getting the education from people that knew more than I did about how to do real estate investing. I had mentors around that would take me by the hand and say, "Let's do this together. Let me show you what I would do." I really gained a lot of confidence out of those types of relationships. It really helped me reduce my fear, so that I could really pull the trigger when it was time to do a transaction.

Shannon:

What are some key attributes that a strong leader in real estate investing should have?

David:

First, being willing to take somebody under your wing. Some people just don't want to do that. They kind of want to do their own thing and they really don't want to give back to the next group or the next generation coming up and share some of their wisdom. I think it's very important to have somebody that's willing to share.

I think another thing that's important is to have somebody that's had the type of success that you want to have in a real estate investing career. They can mentor you about some of the industry pitfalls and the things that didn't work for them. When I am looking for a mentor, I want to make sure that I've got a mentor that is heading down the same path that I want to travel on and that they're a little bit ahead of me. They can bring me along until I've got the comfort and the confidence that I can start to do it on my own. I find myself starting to mentor new real estate investors going through the same kind of thing. I really get a lot of joy out of that because mentors stood up for me when I got started, and now I want to stand up for another batch of new real estate investors and share my wisdom with them and try to help them along and try to reduce some of the bumps along the road.

Shannon:

What type of legacy do you want to leave behind?

David:

I want people to look at their relationship with me and feel that I added something positive to their life, whatever that may be. It could be something as simple as how I did a real estate transaction, or more in depth, how I treated people, which I think is almost more important than the real estate transaction itself. You must treat people with respect and dignity. A lot of people in this country are having some challenging times. If I can make a little impact and reduce that challenge a little bit and steer them into maybe a different possibility for them and open their eyes to creating something for their legacy instead of trading their time for dollars, it will be worth it to me. Most people have a lot more to give than they're really showing right now. A lot of people have really been beaten down over the last 5-10 years, and they stopped dreaming. They just hope they make it until Social Security, or they hope they have their job long enough until they can retire. To have them realize that hope's not a very good strategy, let's start dreaming again. I want to show them what I can do to help inspire them to get their dreams back and to pursue what they're really capable of. That would be a great legacy for me.

James & Lisa Leis

Lisa Leis was born and raised just outside of Cleveland, OH. She was always active in athletics, student government, and, beginning at age 20, doing rehab work on various houses that she lived in. She attended Kent State University where she studied business administration, and then completed her Economics degree at Northwestern University. Soon after, she went to University of Illinois and completed a bachelor's of Nursing. While in college, she rehabbed 3 houses "for fun". Nursing and a love of snow skiing pulled her out west to Park City, UT, where she became a ski instructor and worked at a hospital as an RN in Salt Lake City. Having a passion for traveling, she soon started working as a traveling nurse. While on assignment in northern CA, she fell in love with her environment and has lived in the Sacramento area since 2000, working in pharmaceutical sales and as a clinical educator. Her next rehab was her own house which she lived in for six years, and then converted to a rental income house. Since meeting her husband in 2006 she has become a full-fledged investor and, along with her husband, has developed a local team of investors and has been involved in over 80 real estate deals. Recently, real estate investing has become her full time career and she has retired from nursing.

James Leis was born in Seattle, WA and graduated from Snohomish High School. After high school he joined the Air Force and was an electro-environmental specialist for many different aircrafts such as F-4s, F-16s, OV-10s, A-10s, Awacs, C-5s, and more. He has travelled the world, living in Germany for three years, and seeing places like Holland, Amsterdam, Spain, and France, as well as much of the USA. He made his transfer into real estate so he could focus on being a millionaire. This led him to getting his real estate license, and he owns a real estate brokerage and lending company. He got into real estate investing, and is now a mentor to one of the largest investor communities in Sacramento. He oversees a large nationwide team of investors. His area is broad and includes mentoring, financial literacy, business management, debt reduction, mortgage acceleration, pre-foreclosures, foreclosures, auctions, real estate owning, note buying, wholesaling, and commercial apartment complexes.

James and Lisa Leis have been married for ten years and have one son, Dolan, who is nine-years-old. They currently reside in Sacramento, CA, where they are full time real estate investors.

Contact information
James & Lisa Leis
Lifestyle Dynamics, Inc.
Cashflowgroup@gmail.com

Shannon:

What inspired you to get into real estate?

James:

My background is 20 years of military. I kind of asked a question during the transition, "Where can I make six figures working from home?" I didn't have a degree but I knew that I was good with people. Somebody had suggested that I get my real estate license, so I started studying part-time while still serving in the Air Force, and passed my test a year later. I closed my first transaction while I was still on active duty and got 43% of the commission which was a $7,440 check. I realized that on a part time basis I had just made the equivalent of three months of my military pay. At that point I was hooked. I still had a couple years before I could retire from the military as a 20-year service Vet. I had a couple trips to Iraq following that paycheck so my philosophy and my attitude changed knowing that now I had a plan. At that point,

I wanted out of the military so I could get going with my real estate dreams full-time. I realized that what I was currently doing on a part-time basis would have given me a six-figure income if I were full time. That's what got me hooked on real estate; working part-time and seeing more money coming in.

Shannon:

Lisa, what about you?

Lisa:

I didn't realize I was interested in real estate at first, but thinking back, I've been around the business all my life. When I was little my dad was a plumber and my step-dad was a builder. I got to watch as my step dad put a very large addition on our house, and I went on plumbing jobs with my dad all the time. Also, my neighbor was an architect. I would go hang out at his studio and watch the architects draw. I took an interest in fixing up houses at a young age. My first fixer-upper was when I was in college. I fixed up a house that I was renting. I made suggestions to the owner and he agreed to reimburse me for the cost of the supplies. It was mostly cosmetic: paint, floor sealer, wall paper, etc. I did re-plumb a shower stall once too!

When I was 21 I inherited a house. I fixed up that house and sold it. Had I known a little bit more then, I would have done some things very differently. I bought a condo while I was in college in Chicago. I fixed that up and lived in it for four years and then sold it. Then I bought another house in Utah. That turned into a rental. I ended up going through a bad market fluctuation right after the Olympics in Salt Lake City. My renters flaked on me and I ended up losing it in foreclosure. I'm positive that had I known then what I know now, I wouldn't have lost it. I bought another house in Sacramento, CA. It was originally a Section eight rental. I fixed it up and lived in it for many years. I never connected making a business out of my hobby though, until I met James. I started to get educated on how to actually make a business out of all my fix up skills. The house in Sacramento has now become one of our best cash flow properties.

James:
The reason that property became such a great income producer is because we were successful in getting a principal reduction on it.

Lisa:
Yes, we did a principal reduction which was practically unheard of. But because the education taught us the subtle tricks and negotiation skills, we were able to leverage our knowledge and we turned a mortgage modification into an approved principal reduction. We were able to completely eliminate a second mortgage loan of $50,000, and the new principal loan went from the original purchase price of $240,000 to $117,000 (which was current market value). If our education wasn't as good as it was, I don't think we would have pulled off like that.

A mortgage modification takes an existing loan that's on the house and adjusts it for a new payment at a different interest rate. You still have the original principal, the original debt on the house, but you're adjusting for a better payment to keep your house.

James:

We were at $301,000 on the mortgage. That dropped down to $117,000 at a 2.75% interest rate. The second, which was $50,000, got dropped and just sent us a re-conveyance, which means it was paid off or just let go.

Lisa:

At the time there were government programs that basically allowed us to wipe that debt off in order to be able to save our home. We knew what our rights were and what the programs were because we were getting educated. We were able to leverage that and use that to get the second mortgage wiped away. Our original payment had gone as high as $2,200 a month. After everything was said and done our final payment with principal, interest, taxes and insurance ended up being $680 a month.

Shannon:

Did you guys continue to live there or did you rent that out?

James:

We lived in it for a few more years. We found a lender that only had the qualifications of living there one year. In about a little over a year and a half we put our finances back in order and business bounced back, we were able to qualify for our dream house that we live in now.

Lisa:

We lived in it for as long as it was required by the terms of the modification.

James:

Now the rental income is $670 a month above our payment.

Shannon:

Is a principal reduction and a short sale similar?

Lisa:

No, because the principal reduction doesn't affect your credit. It was a special government-backed program at the time. What happened was that initially they did not do the paperwork correctly on the modification in a timely manner to meet the requirements of what that certain program was. They tried to cancel my modification and I called them out on it. I said to them, "You know, you guys dropped the ball on this. I got everything in on time. What are you going to do to fix it?" They took a look at our income and came back with, "The original program is no longer available, but you actually qualify for the principal reduction program that just started."

James:
A short sale is a strategy that is looking to pay down a loan amount vs current market value. If a home owner is over-leveraged on the mortgage and they need to get rid of a property for various reasons, the investor will work with the home owner to make an offer to the bank for a settlement payoff. Someone other than the owner or immediate family is investing or buying the house by 'shorting' the banks on what the actual loan payoff amount is. Then the bank is going to write off the remaining debt. That remaining debt may or may not be accounted for on the home seller's tax burden. It's up to the bank. Short Sale is a strategy of acquisition not a strategy for a homeowner who wants to keep their property. A homeowner strategy would be to either apply for a loan modification or a principal reduction.

Lisa:
Actually, the short sale still puts a blemish on your credit report because it reports that you had to write off the mortgage. Whereas, what we did with the principal reduction did not blemish our credit report.

Shannon:
Do you currently acquire homes via the short sale strategy?

James:
Yeah. It's my favorite strategy.

Lisa:

It takes patience to wait for the final transaction to complete, but you usually get the best price and the best potential for profit. We have one right now that is up in Lake Tahoe, CA. We have an accepted offer from the owner and we are waiting for the bank's final acceptance. This is going to be a fun one because it will be both for rental and our own use. We will have equity of over $100,000 that can then be leveraged into other investments.

Shannon:

James, do you find that it is helpful that you have your real estate license when investing?

James:

When I first got started, I had my license, but as soon as I got my education and started building teams by supporting and mentoring other people, I let my real estate license lapse. I let it go because there were so many people on my team that have their license, that I found my role being more of a conductor than musician.

Lisa:

I want to let people know that being a real estate agent and being a real estate investor is like comparing a dog to a cat. Being an agent you learn about the transaction and the real estate laws. Being an investor means learning about the strategies for making a profit from the transaction and managing a business that will continue to create passive income.

James:

A license just allows you to write contracts and complete a sale.

I got out of being an agent and went to the investor side because the investor side adds an entirely different component. You control your own time. You're not controlled by clients. You're buying the market for yourself at a discount. You find it. You get to control it and you use other people's money to fund it. Then you put it into rehab or the contractor's work. Then you let the realtors do their job and sell it. From my standpoint, I like to have more family time and I have less stress. The only stress in there is to be able to manage the monthly debt payment between start to profit.

I do see some value in an agent-investor /husband-wife team. If a couple can work together and put those two skills together, they could really do some great stuff.

Shannon:

Do you think a husband/wife team can be just as successful without that?

James:

Yes, you can be successful with or without that combo.

What agents don't know is what I call the four I's. They don't know the income tax, how to get around the whole entire tax strategy. They don't realize that the interest from all of the mortgages are amortized so they're helping people really get in debt and stay in debt and really helping the banking systems. The agents really don't understand return on investment because they're not in that field of investing and really understanding return on investment.

The last one is insurance. How are they protecting themselves so they keep peace of mind? The agent is doing their job on a commission basis. You can make your money there. The investing side, when you understand the how-to, and Garrett Gunderson taught me this, the five steps to financial freedom is recovering cash. Agents don't know how to recover cash.

Lisa:

I think one of the key factors is that it's good in terms of a dynamic or synergy effect between someone who is primarily an investor and someone who is an agent. It may be good in terms of being able to look up or find properties or whatnot but the thing with investors you have to remember is that one of their primary strategies is finding things off-market before it hits the real estate agent's table or desk. That's one of the key strategies that investors learn; how to find those properties before they even make it to the MLS with the real estate agent.

Shannon:

How can they do that?

James:

A great listing agent who makes a lot of money finding great off-market properties would be a perfect investor, but most of them will tell me they don't have the money to buy the properties they're listing. They don't have the leverage of a team, but if they are good at finding properties they're usually only making the small commissions instead of the big profits. They haven't had that financial literacy to go out there and get their clients out of debt. I help them understand that a great listing agent would be a perfect investor if only they knew the components of wealth building.

Shannon:

How do you guys recommend that people find these great deals off-market? If off-market were that easy wouldn't everybody be doing it?

James:

Yes. That's the easiest component once you start your team. I don't find my own properties. I build a team. All the books for real estate investing say you've got to build your team, build your team, build your team. I build my team by helping people understand how to get out of debt and the more I can help people learn, the better I do. Eventually they might go off on their own, but that's okay too, it means I did a good job.

Word of mouth and listening and teaching is the best way to build a good reputation that will bring you business. Everyone in your phone contacts should know what you do, and how you can help people.

Lisa:

One of the people we've worked with who was in a distressed situation has now gone on to become one of our most active, successful investors. They became educated and learned the strategies and now they're off doing their own investing.

James:

Now they're helping other people.

Lisa:

Essentially, they're paying it forward.

James:

Yes. It is a huge paying it forward concept. That's how we continue to expand not only locally but nationwide because family members know other family members in other states.

Shannon:

Do you guys do anything with multi-family homes?

Lisa:

As a matter of fact, I called about an assisted living home listing yesterday. I'm waiting on numbers right now to evaluate it. I have a special interest in senior assisted living situations and helping out with that market because of my background in nursing. I've noticed while working in the nursing field that there are not enough quality assisted living home options for families to choose from.

James:

And as for me, veteran housing is an interest since I'm a 20-year retired Air Force vet. Veteran housing is the next phase in our purpose-driven life.

Right now I'm focused in Kansas City and we have a couple other markets we're looking into but right now, the Kansas City numbers work. It's really profitable but you have to have a really good team on the ground when working remote, you really have to know what you're doing and have had some hands on experience.

Lisa:

We have people out there and feelers out in multiple states throughout the country. Between Florida, DC area, Kansas, Washington State and Ohio.

James:

We're looking at numbers after rehab of $30,000 to $40,000. That puts people into home ownership and renting around the $700, $800, $900 mark. We've got one property that was acquired for $35,000. It's a 2,500 square foot home and has a good tenant. Currently it rents for $800/month. That's a really good number for a buy and hold. If you don't have a team on the ground, you're not going to be able to put these kinds of numbers together.

Shannon:

How do you propose that people build a strong team? What do you think the number one thing is that you have to have within your team for it to be successful?

James:

A great mentor.

We've had a great mentor from the start, and we keep getting mentors for various areas of our life and business as we grow. When we start new projects we have to pull from a whole variety of resources and knowledge bases. Our mentors help us put the plan together to make sure it's in line with the overall goal. There are a lot of people involved in each project. Having the right team and the knowledge to guide your team is what will make you wealthy. For example, most people think that a financial planner is going to make you wealthy, but they only have one side of the coin when it comes to wealth creation. They just don't know what they don't know, so the more educated you are personally, the more you can guide your finances toward your goals. When we started in this business we had a tax person that had us structured all wrong and missed over $10,000 in returns. He thought he knew how to work with us since he used to work for the IRS and I'm sure he meant well, but he just didn't know what we had learned.

Building a team for wealth creation is so critical. But it has to be the right fit for you and your goals, and there has to be a willingness to communicate among team members to make sure the common goal is understood. You have to know that one person can't do it all.

When you build your team you're building a team around wealth creation. You might find one person that's really good at finding properties. You say, great, that's what you do. Because of their lack of knowledge regarding how to find funding, you're going to add them to your team and you're going to make more money for both you and that person because they just want to find properties. This is what's really interesting, not everyone wants to do it all. You've got to vet and really look at how you build your team around all areas in real estate investing.

What is the best piece of advice anybody has ever given to you in real estate investing?

Lisa:
Don't get emotionally connected to the property. You have to hold back your personal preferences and remember to not evaluate the property on your own likes. It's the numbers that matter.

Shannon:
James, what's the best piece of advice that anybody's ever given to you or is it the same?

James:
There have been so many pieces of advice but I would say after going through the process of coming out of the military to create a path to being a millionaire, my thought is, "choose the life you want and then align your plan accordingly."

Lisa:
Set your goals and work backwards.

James:
Yes, Set your goals and work backwards. We help people create a plan based on their goals. It's all about what they want. Quite often though, people are inspired by the lifestyle that we live now. My biggest piece of advice is you can't have security and freedom, they are two completely different value systems in the same niche.

Shannon:

What is your sole purpose in life and the legacy that you want to leave behind?

James:

My wife, number one, inspired me to just keep going along the dream path. My number two is to make sure my 13-year-old knows that he can do anything he wants. He saw me do my first fix and flip and saw me get a $237,000 check. He was sitting at a table and I asked him, "What do you want to do when you grow up?" He said, "You just made more money than my teacher. I'm learning a different philosophy." He wanted freedom and he's really going through this education in high school. I didn't want to be the parent that said, "Go to school and get good grades so you'll get a good job." I wanted to be the parent that says, "Live the life that you deserve to have by the choices you make. What do you want?" That is changing the next generation. That is my core purpose as I believe everybody's been told these philosophies and myths and rules that don't govern the lifestyle that people deserve or want to have.

Lisa:

I have kind of a similar philosophy. I have never been an inside the box type of person, even at a young age.

There's so much exciting stuff outside that box.

You can still have a foot a little bit in the box but explore what's out there. Explore your options and see what's out there and available. If there is something that people have been told it's that there's a restriction of money or there are restrictions and limitations but there's not. Take a look out here. You still have that box available but you explore and see what's outside there.

Anjanette Mickelsen

Entrepreneur, Educator, Coach, Singer, Songwriter, and Freedom Enthusiast

As a real estate investor and mentor, Anjanette has earned the nickname the "Queen of Cashflow". She is respected nationwide for her Cashflow board game trainings, which teach the basics of financial literacy and real estate investing. She has given Cashflow trainings in Salt Lake City, Las Vegas, and Oahu. She proudly serves on the leadership team of Elevate, one of the nation's fastest growing real estate investing communities. Anjanette loves to help educate others about financial literacy and real estate investing to produce passive income. Some of her favorite subjects include saving money on taxes, debt mastery, credit management, interest reduction, and mortgage & debt acceleration.

Mickelsen's real estate business has blessed her with the ability to follow a lifelong passion as a world class vocal coach. She trains and coaches successful singers across the globe, from her hometown in the Salt Lake City area to long distance clients over the internet. She is the youngest teacher in the world to receive the highest certification level from Speech Level Singing, a ten-year process. She has taught at the prestigious VocalizeU Summer Vocal Program, and trained students and teachers as a Mentor Instructor in the Institute of Vocal Advancement. Her clients have become successful and professional artists, received scholarships and awards, and made top categories on American Idol. Songwriting credits includes artists such as GENTRI, Hilary Weeks, Madilyn Paige, and Lexi Walker.

Contact Info:
anjanettewithelevate@gmail.com
Music Website: www.thesingingpro.com

Shannon:
What inspired you to get into real estate?

Anjanette:
My passion for music inspired me to get into real estate. I'm a professional singing coach and songwriter, and have been pursuing these passions for almost 20 years. It's been a blast. When I first started learning how to teach voice and write songs, I knew it was a non-traditional path to financial stability. Although this path was rife with challenges, I was excited by the benefits—being my own boss, and doing what I love.

I started doing research, and discovered that there's basically two things that financially free people do. First, they own a profitable business, and second they invest in real estate. I didn't have a clue about real estate investing back then, so I had to spend many hours conducting research.

One of the best ways I educated myself about real estate investing was playing a board game called Cashflow. This game completely changed my life. It teaches the basics of financial literacy and real estate investing. The more you play that game, the more you realize, "If I can get these basics down, I can do this in real life. If I can do this in real life, then I can set myself financially free."

I realized I would have to invest in real estate to secure myself financially as I pursued my passion for music.

Shannon:
What is the most creative way you've acquired a property?

Anjanette:
Let me talk about intellectual property, for a second. This is where music is actually very similar to real estate investing. For me as a songwriter, I have the opportunity to create intellectual property. I write songs for artists or bands that are going to produce that music and turn it into a product. Every time those artists sell that music, I make money through royalties.

I have a passion for creating intellectual property through song writing, and my other passion is real estate investing. Both have the benefit of creating passive income.

Shannon:
What is passive income?

Anjanette:
Passive income is a form of income that comes from an asset. The investor's definition of an asset is anything that generates revenue. It's a really important distinction to understand. What most people think is an asset is not actually an asset. For example, people think that their home is an asset because it's something of value. However, your home never puts income into your pocket. Even if you have the mortgage paid off, it's still taking money out of your pocket. You have to pay for repairs, insurance, taxes, etc. It's always going to be something that takes away from you, even though it's something of value.

I find it helps to think of intellectual property as something that is tangible, even if it's not. When somebody buys a song from iTunes, it's adding value into their lives and people are willing to pay money for it. Right?

Shannon:
Right.

Anjanette:
Because I wrote that song, and then somebody else produced that song, there are streams of income that come when people buy the song. Passive income is cool because it comes from an asset that you worked hard on one time, and then it pays you for the rest of your life.

Whether "it" is a song or a house, "it" has to become something that becomes a passive form of income for it to become financially profitable. Obviously songwriting is a wonderful thing, whether or not people hear it, or it becomes successful enough to become income. However, when it does produce income, it becomes something that is very financially viable and powerful. It's the same thing with real estate. It's not a good deal unless it's bringing money in.

Something that board game taught me is you can talk to an appraiser and they can tell you, "Oh my gosh, if you just replaced the water heater, painted the fence and weeded the lawn and blah,

blah, blah." However, unless the market conditions and the way that you bought the house allow that property to generate revenue and put money into your pocket every single month, it's not a good deal.

Shannon:
Where do you find this board game, Cashflow?

Anjanette:
It is a board game created by Sharon Lechter and Robert Kiyosaki. You can find copies of it on Amazon for around $65. I get to do Cashflow trainings on a frequent basis, which is one of my favorite ways to teach about real estate. We have a whole bunch of board games set up, and we start by explaining the rules of the game. We teach people some basic principles about real estate investing and how to read a financial statement through the board game. It's really fun and an easy way for people to start learning the basics. Once they learn the basics, people start believing in themselves and start understanding, "Hey, this is something I can do in real life."

Shannon:
Do you feel that real estate investing has changed your life?

Anjanette:
Absolutely. It has changed the way that I see money, the way that I see my relationships with people. It has helped me to understand that the way to create financial freedom for yourself is by helping to solve other people's problems.

Shannon:
How do you solve other people's problems by being a real estate investor?

Anjanette:
Often times people get into financial situations that they can't get themselves out of. Maybe somebody lost their job and they're getting a few months behind on their mortgage. Maybe there was a death in the family and the inheritors of the property don't know what to

do with the property, or are having a hard time selling the property. Maybe there's a dispute between the siblings and they can't get those things figured out. If you have the knowledge to solve people's problems, you can find great deals on real estate properties that will turn into revenue generating assets.

Shannon:

In your business, do you do more rentals or fix and flips?

Anjanette:

I personally do more passive income, because I love what I do in the music business, so I'm never going to stop doing that.

That produces income for me. It helps to produce a little bit more cash flow. What I need more of in my financial strategy are those passive income producing assets. They work without me having to put much time or effort into them.

Shannon:

Do you do all of your investing locally or do you have national investments as well?

Anjanette:

As of right now, I do it on a more local level. Locally first and eventually I will expand nationally.

Shannon:

Why would you use a lease option with a potential buyer versus just selling them the property?

Anjanette:

It depends on the needs of the person who is purchasing the property. For example, if they don't have the credit to get the loan or the funding that they need to buy the property outright, a lease option could be a great solution. They just need to put down some option money on the property to secure it for the next year or two. During this time, they build their credit so they can finance a loan. It's a great thing for you because you've got a committed tenant interested in homeownership instead of renters that might come in and trash the place. These are people that are wanting that property for a home. They're going to take good care of it, they're going to pay you on time, and they're going to do everything that they can to put themselves in a position to buy the property from you.

Shannon:

If someone is doing a lease option, do they have the right to, say, remodel the kitchen?

Anjanette:

Each contract is different but usually, no. Since they are renting the property, with an option to buy at a specific time in the future they are usually not responsible for taking care of the property, nor allowed to make changes or improvements. The easiest way for a seller to accommodate the buyer in a case like this is to have the renter put down a larger deposit to cover any changes.

Shannon:

What is a seller financed deal, and why is it a benefit to you, as an investor?

Anjanette:

Seller financing is a fantastic strategy for investors. Seller financed notes are an asset I find very interesting. It's basically owning the paper side of real estate, and it's similar to intellectual property. He who owns the paper owns the income.

Shannon:

Have you had a situation where you had a car loan with a company, and then you get a notice in the mail that tells you, "Hey, your loan on this car got sold to another company, so start making your payments to that other company." Have you ever had that experience before?

Anjanette:

I have had that experience before.

All that happened is the original company that gave you the loan for your car sold the paper or the debt on the car to another company. The benefit for them is they were able to get almost all of the money up front for that loan sooner than later, and it's a benefit to the buyer of the paper because they now are making that monthly passive income from me paying my car loan each month.

Shannon:
Is that similar to a wholesaling agent?

Anjanette:
It's a little bit different than wholesaling, which is when you find a property for an investor who wants to do a fix and flip or a rental. You negotiate with the seller and get it under contract with an assignable clause. This means that you're going to control the contract, and then sell it to another investor. If you can't find another investor in the time frame stipulated in the contract, you've got an escape clause so you don't actually have to be responsible for the property. You then sell the contract for that property to another investor for a finder's fee.

Shannon:
Is it the same as buying a note?

Anjanette:
That's a little bit different. With seller financed notes, you are either buying the paper on a property that will give you passive income each month, or you broker the note to other investors who have a different investing criteria than you. Seller financed notes can be a hybrid. You can do massive income with seller financed notes, as well as passive income.

Shannon:
What happens if you do a seller financed deal and the seller defaults on the loan, even though you're paying them?

Anjanette:
Well, in many seller financed deals, they already own the property

outright, so in a sense they are acting like the bank. They may not have a mortgage or note to default on from their perspective. Their concern is making sure that the person renting, leasing, or buying their home makes their monthly payments.

The nice thing about real estate is that if somebody defaults and you've done your job correctly, there are ways to foreclose on a property or to have something that's collateral or securing the deal.

Shannon:

Do you think that real estate investing success is dependent on a strong economy?

Anjanette:

No. The reason for that is very simple. People will always need a place to live. You will always have a need for shelter. It doesn't matter whether the economy is good or bad. There's always going to be a need for it and therefore there's always going to be a way to make money at it.

Shannon:

Do you think that your investment strategy should change based on whether you are in a strong economy or a weak economy?

Anjanette:

This is what people need to understand if they want to stop living paycheck to paycheck. Many people think that the way to make money in real estate, or any other investment vehicle for that matter, is when the economy is going up. However, for people who are educated, people who understand how real estate works, they know you can make money in any economic situation. The key is to know what type of strategy to use. This also applies to the parts of the country that you are investing in because each is going to have different market conditions.

Shannon:

Is that why people invest nationally, so that it diversifies their portfolio?

Anjanette:

Absolutely. To give you an example, I have a friend in Oahu, Hawaii who lives the good life on the beach with his family, but the majority of his real estate investing is in the Midwest. Why? Because they are passive income producing properties that better fit his investing criteria. They're harder to find on Hawaii.

Hawaii has extremely expensive real estate, so it can be more difficult to find properties that make sense for a cash flow or passive income strategy. You have to raise more capital to invest in those deals, but if you can find cheaper properties with more bang for your buck, why wouldn't you invest in those deals?

Shannon:

Pretend somebody came to you and said, "I really want to get started doing what you're doing, but I don't have any money and my credit is horrible." What are some strategies or advice you would give them so they could also get into real estate investing?

Anjanette:

I would say to them, "Fantastic! That's great!" The reason I say this is because the majority of people who get started in real estate don't have any money or credit. This means that they have to get themselves educated, so that when they're structuring their real estate deals, they have the knowledge to make that deal happen. People think that the hardest part about real estate investing is finding the money, but it's actually the easiest.

Shannon:

Oh, how so?

Anjanette:

You have to understand that if you don't have the money and you don't have the credit, you're going to have to partner with somebody who does have those resources. You've got to have something else to bring to the table that they need or want.

An ideal partnership is if an investor has money but they don't want to do the work, and you have no money, but you're willing to do the work.

That's the ideal partnership because people who have lots of money are often tired of working. They've probably been working their whole life to acquire that money.

They value their time. This means they need somebody to do the work so they can have their freedom and ensure their investment is generating a good return.

Shannon:
What do you think are the most important values that a real estate investor should have?

Anjanette:
The ability to create great relationships. Every real estate strategy demands you find buyers and sellers. You've got to be able to make connections with people, which means being likable, personable, and trustworthy. People will do business with those that they like and trust. It's the same thing in music or in theater. You could have everything that they're looking for — the right look, the right sound — but if you're really difficult to work with, you're not going to get the job. It's not worth their time or hassle. If you've not likeable or trustworthy, then this is going to be a business that you struggle with.

Shannon:
In your real estate business, have you had any specific mentors that have really helped you navigate potential pitfalls?

Anjanette:
Oh yeah, absolutely. I'm so lucky to be part of a local real estate investment community. These guys have been absolutely invaluable helping me take my first steps in real estate investing. I come from the music business, which has a completely different language. While it's not a completely different set of skills, there's some things that are very different. Having their experience and expertise guide me through that process has been invaluable.

Shannon:

Are you currently mentoring anyone?

Anjanette:

Yes, I'm helping to advise some people in Hawaii, Salt Lake City, Utah and Las Vegas and will likely be moving my way into Denver, as well.

Shannon:

What type of legacy do you want to leave behind?

Anjanette:

I want to leave a legacy of freedom and financial literacy. Real estate investing, songwriting, or anything else you do to generate income should be about helping to free up your time. That way you can spend more time with your loved ones and pursuing your dreams. If you are always trading your time for dollars, you will never become the person that you want. You will have regrets that will haunt you for the rest of your life. No one is going to care about punching a time-card at a job that you didn't care about. You've got to free up your time so you can do what you were put on this earth to do.

I have discovered from working with this community and educating myself in this process that what most people think about money is not true. When you understand how money actually works, it becomes a wonderful tool in your life to facilitate many good things. One of the biggest problems in our country is that most people think they know about money, but are completely financially illiterate. Traditional education is not preparing us to be financially successful. We are just being taught how to be employees. We need to be responsible for educating ourselves to be financially successful. If we learn how to become creators of opportunities rather than consumers of jobs, we can completely change how this country works. People could completely change their lifestyles and determine if they are in freedom or financial bondage for the rest of their lives.

Whether I am helping somebody invest in real estate or working as a professional vocal coach, I am helping people become the best version of themselves that they possibly can be.

Chris Neugent

Chris Neugent is a native of Dallas, TX and a Marine Corps Veteran of OEF (Operation Enduring Freedom). Honorably discharged after 6 years of service he pursued his passion to become a Real Estate Investor. Since then, he has helped grow a team of over 100 investors and also been a part of numerous transactions. His future plans in real estate are to acquire high-rise commercial properties in Downtown Dallas.

Contact Info:
Email: ChrisNeugent@TheREIJunkie.com
Social Media: www.Facebook.com/TheChrisNeugent

Shannon:

What inspired you to get into real estate?

Chris:

Before I started real estate investing, I enlisted in the United States Marine Corps for 6 years and during this time, I was deployed to Afghanistan as a part of Operation Enduring Freedom.

I knew that I didn't want to have a boss or work for someone else when I completed my service. In the military there is always someone above you in your chain of command.

I didn't know exactly how I was going to do that until my wife Princess dragged me out to a real estate seminar! That opened my mind to a whole new way of thinking. Real estate is the one thing I feel does it all for me... flexibility, freedom, and a sense of purpose. I understood why I should do real estate but I still didn't know how.

Shannon:

When your wife dragged you out, were you worried at all about the income or did you just trust her?

Chris:

I definitely trusted her, and I trusted my gut... I just didn't know what to expect, which was a little intimidating. But I've always been adventurous and open-minded. However, I did wonder if this was something I could actually do.

Shannon:

According to Forbes magazine, real estate is one of the 3 ways people become wealthy. Why do you feel like real estate is one of the best ways to accomplish this goal? Second, why is wealth important?

Chris:

Well, real estate is tangible. It's an asset that won't go away. If you buy a car, obviously it's depreciating and doesn't actively make you money. If you drive it every so often, keep it serviced, in pristine condition, sell it 50 years later, and the market just so happens to have a demand for your exact car, then you might just be able to make some money. With real estate, it's one of the 3 basic human needs—food, water and shelter. Someone will always need it no matter what, and the value will always be there.

Wealth is value; I'm only as important as the value I bring to this world. So wealth is important to me because it directly relates to the value I consistently bring to others. I'll know I'm wealthy when the value I bring to others exceeds past my living days.

I want my daughter, her name's Madison, to understand the principles of wealth in relation to real estate. No matter what she decides to do in life, I want her to always look to create value for herself and others. If she lives with good intentions, everything she wants in life will be at her fingertips. Another example: my mother, Greta, used to teach me how to balance a checkbook, so I want to take that lesson and evolve it into how to maintain a balance sheet. Being able to pass my knowledge and passion down to my daughter, the way my mother did for me, is one of the things that drives me every day.

Shannon:

If you're starting with little money or poor credit, what are some things people can do to get into real estate?

Chris:

The first thing they have to do is seek out someone that's willing to help them. They simply must seek out a mentor, friend, or even a family member that has their best interest at heart, much like my mentor John Ferguson has been to me. Find someone that knows what you need to know and study his or her every move. Always be willing to earn your stripes, and someone will invest their time and money to see you succeed.

Shannon:

How important do you feel that it is to have a great mentor?

Chris:

It's absolutely crucial with anything we do in life—sports, education, even learning how to drive. It takes someone with the experience, the knowledge, and the know-how to pass those tools on. Now, there are individuals that do it on their own, but it may take years, tons of capital, and loads of frustration to figure out what they could have learned in mere minutes from someone else's experiences.

Shannon:

Why do you feel that people sometimes fail at real estate? Do you think it has anything to do with whether or not they have a team or they're alone?

Chris:

People fail at real estate because they underestimate what they need to truly succeed in this business: the knowledge, the team, the cash, and the systems. I truly feel like I would have failed in this business if I hadn't had someone guiding me throughout the process. My success will always be attributed to all of the individuals that have helped me get to the point that I am now.

Shannon:

What do you feel is most crucial when building a team?

Chris:

Diversity. We have a great variety of people here in Dallas, and I think it works in our favor. It's not crucial that each individual be a great real estate investor. Some of us are great with the numbers and negotiations; others are great with contracting and supervising projects. It's nice to have a diverse group of individuals because everyone has different opinions, ideas, and perspectives. As long as the collective is clear on the end goal, it makes for some well-thought-out strategies and makes for a great real estate investor team.

Shannon:

Do you have a favorite group meeting you've had with your investor team that you'd like to share some of the ideas from?

Chris:

I'll share one of my favorites. Last Christmas, we were all sitting around a u-shaped table as we put together gingerbread houses. John bought a bunch of gingerbread houses we could put together, and so we made it into a team competition. We all split up into groups—Husbands and wives split into different groups. It was a challenge to see who, within a specified time, could create the most unique property with gingerbread houses.

John didn't tell us why we were doing it, but instead, it needed to be unique. In the end, it all sort of gave us an interesting perspective regarding what some of our creative thinking could turn into. "Where do we put the jelly bean? Where do we put the peppermints? How do you use the icing?" All these questions were suddenly important. In seeing that, you literally got to see people's ideas come to life. And we really started to see their passions. This is why it's so great to have a group to lean on. All of the different perspectives that come from it are great.

Shannon:
What is your favorite part about real estate investing?

Chris:
My favorite part is the comradery. When I was in the Marine Corps, all we had were our brothers and sisters to the left and to the right of us. That's exactly what I have here. That's what keeps me going. I don't just go about this business thinking only of myself. I'm constantly and always thinking about all the team members and what type of value I can bring to the group and to others.

Shannon:
Do you have a favorite acquisition strategy?

Chris:
I love short sales. They are a headache, but they are my favorite way to acquire a property.

Shannon:
What do you anticipate when doing a short sale and how long does it usually take from beginning to end?

Chris:

With a short sale I typically anticipate it to take 6-9 months just depending on the bank and negotiations. I know that when BPO and appraisers come out to walk the property, take pictures, and run their estimates, it can either go really quickly or take quite some time. It's also a "hurry up and wait" game with the bank. Meaning, anything the bank needs, we have to hurry it over. But if we, the investors, need anything from the bank, we have to wait.

Shannon:

It's kind of an ironic name, "short sale."

Chris:

Yes, very.

Shannon:

Why do you feel like short sales are such a good investment?

Chris:

Typically, at the discounted purchase price, you'll see a decent size return on investment with a short sale. Whether the home needs a ton of rehab or hardly any cosmetic work, the bank is more times than none willing to work with an all cash buyer versus letting it sit and cost them more money by foreclosing. Either way, the home-owner is still in a much better financial position because of the short sale and will have more options to work with in the long run.

Shannon:

Why is that important to you?

Chris:

I take pride in helping people. I also learned that from my mother. If I'm not out there creating a change for individuals and helping them in a positive way, then I need to change what I'm doing.

Shannon:

How does completing a short sale help all parties involved?

Chris:

The best way I can help someone is by letting him or her know that a foreclosure isn't the only answer. In many cases, a short sale can be negotiated on the behalf of the homeowner, and this short sale is the purchase of a property short of what is owed to the bank; so in other words, a discounted sale. I myself have had to go through a short sale, and I can tell you, it's a scary thing thinking the bank is about to take your home in a foreclosure and there's no turning back. When the bank decides to take the home from a homeowner, what type of services are provided to them to get them back on their feet? None. The least I can do is help someone feel at ease while staying rent-free during the 6-9 months of negotiations with the bank. That gives them time to find employment, time to find a better place to live, and a head start moving forward in life. The homeowner doesn't have to come out of pocket. I bring all money to the table to get the bank off their back. I'll see a return on my investment later because, not only did I help a family facing foreclosure, but I also fixed up that home and was able to provide it for another family. It's a win-win for all parties involved.

Most foreclosures have a negative impact on credit for 7 years. If the bank agrees on a short sale, the homeowner's credit is only impacted for about 3 years. Anyone facing a situation where their credit is going to be hurt would feel at ease knowing that they will be able to move past a credit ding faster.

Having the ability to help others is great, but especially when it's a member of my own family. Recently, I worked with a short sale that was actually acquired through a family member of mine who has since passed. They didn't know what to do, and they didn't know what their options were. I was just getting into the business myself, so I was seeking out different individuals who could help. Once I presented the property to John and Gavin, two of my mentors, they were more than happy to assist with taking the lead, getting all of the documentation together, negotiating with the bank, and making sure the appointments were set. I was able to walk potential buyers through the property and make sure that questions were being answered, and then, I actively reported all of this back to John and Gavin.

And we're finishing it up now. The bank has just submitted their offer, and they want $25,000 for this property. The property is worth a minimum of $40,000 in the area, and it only needs about $5,000 in renovations. We'll actually be figuring out a strategy for one of the investors on the team to acquire it.

This situation was sad, but it was also great that I was able to help my family and keep their trust while making a profit for myself and other investors. With anything I do, I always give my word that I'll find a solution to get it done.

Shannon:
How important is to you to stay true to your word?

Chris:
That's all we have as human beings. We constantly build relationships based off our word, our bond. With that said, if an individual cannot be trusted, that individual can never provide any true, unquestionable value to anyone, because you never really know what their true motive may be.

Shannon:
Since there are so many parties involved, do you find that, in real estate, it's easy to stay true to your word?

Chris:
It's easy for me because I will never break my standards. I've run into those type of people who don't have morals. In real estate, everything an individual does is directly represented either by documentation, word of mouth, or just relationships, period. I pride myself on making sure I'm always telling the truth and being upfront with individuals. A rule of thumb I live by to protect myself is "trust but verify."

Shannon:
How has real estate investing changed your life?

Chris:

I feel like I can truly reach my life goals by doing what I'm doing now. Traditional schooling didn't give me the knowledge, training, and the mentorship I have now. These are the true tools every person, no matter the business, needs to succeed.

Shannon:

Where do you see your team growing?

Chris:

In the next 10 years, I plan on us having well over 5,000 investors across the nation. I see us taking this across the globe, and I really feel we'll do so if we keep working.

My potential future team members are regular people just like you and me. They don't necessarily like where they've been currently heading in life. Yet, they're real go-getters even though they don't have all the support to get them going. They're tired of their broke family members telling them they can't do it. These type of people are literally everywhere we look. We walk by people every day that look like life has knocked them down one last time. They are always looking for an opportunity to just get out of their dead end job and travel the world not having to worry. I want them to mirror myself. If they are truly serious about making a change, being trustworthy, dependable, and have a passion for helping others, then they have the qualities I'm looking for.

Shannon:

Where are you going to find these investors?

Chris:

I've collaborated with my wife and mentor on using social media as one route. Since we've started to see the shift in everyone's focus as far as branding and advertising, I know this avenue is the best to find those individuals who are seeking out a better way of life. If you look up, you'll notice everyone looking down at his or her smart devices. It's remarkable how we've really evolved on every level with all the different communication platforms. Future investors are evolving in this new world too. Media and content are now accessible at the click of finger. The better I am at understanding that avenue then the better my businesses will become, not least of which because I can tap that future talent. In our day and age, if you don't have any sort of social media, your business will have to work twice as hard to pull in only half the business of someone who is using it.

Shannon:

What is your favorite social media outlet for real estate investing?

Chris:

Facebook is probably number one, but I truly like them all. On Facebook, however, you get pictures, comments, likes, and videos. If done the right way, your Facebook can be a one-stop shop for your prospects!

I also see the most returns from Facebook. But it's a ton of work to really get traction vs. the other outlets.

Shannon:

Do you have goals for how many followers you'd like to have?

Chris:

Ultimately, I would like to have 1,000,000 followers on my Facebook. You usually see that, at the level, your voice can be heard, and for the value I want to bring to the world, I would need at least that many followers.

Shannon:

What advice would you give to someone who is allowing fear to hold them back from starting in real estate investing?

Chris:

Take a leap of faith. Trust in yourself and realize that everything you've ever done in life, you were once scared to do. Whether it was to go to high school or trying out for varsity basketball, you took that leap. Take that leap now. The last thing you'll ever want to do is regret not giving it a try. And really, if you had one life to live, what would you do with it?

Shannon:

What type of legacy do you want to leave?

Chris:

I want people to remember me as the purest form of what a human is supposed to be. Trustworthy, dependable, kind, funny, and just always being selfless. I think that sort of legacy will live on versus how much money I have or how many properties I've owned. I just want to go out with a bang. I want my family to be proud. I want hundreds of millions of individuals whose lives I've touched to say, "That man was a great man."

Dr. Malaika Singleton

Dr. Malaika Singleton is the founder and CEO of Singleton Investments and CEO of the Saint Nia Foundation, Inc. A neuroscientist by training, she spent over five years in state government policy and programs as a Science and Technology Policy Fellow for the California Council on Science and Technology (CCST), as well as a consultant for the California State Senate and Program Coordinator/Analyst for the California Alzheimer's Disease Centers. After being on the traditional path of higher education and W-2 employment, she was left longing for autonomy, time freedom, and financial independence, prompting her to begin a career in financial literacy and real estate investment education.

The mission of Singleton Investments is to share key financial literacy concepts, education programs, business/investment opportunities, support/mentorship, and resources to solve financial problems and empower others to achieve their goals. The mission of the Saint Nia Foundation is to prepare young people (ages 12-18 and, for youth in foster care, up to 21) for financial independence and success in all areas of their lives. Dr. Singleton volunteered with the foundation for nine years before taking over as CEO in 2015. She holds a bachelor's degree in biology and psychology, jointly awarded by Rutgers University-Newark College of Arts and Sciences and the New Jersey Institute of Technology, and a doctorate in neuroscience from the University of California, Davis.

Contact Info:
Email: singletoninvestments1@gmail.com
http://www.singleton-investments.com
http://singletoninvestments.we-do-realestate.com
https://www.facebook.com/SingletonInvestments

Shannon:

What inspired you to get into real estate?

Malaika:

My family is one of my biggest inspirations. Many of my ancestors started purchasing land in the 1870s in South Carolina, where I grew up. I was raised in a culture of self-sufficiency. People were investing in raw land for farming and building homes with very little knowledge and with the resources they had. My parents were real estate investors so they were landlords for most of their lives and have continued to purchase property. It just seemed natural to invest in real estate, but I wanted to make sure that I did it right.

Shannon:

Would you say that your parents have been instrumental in helping you now that you do have more knowledge?

Malaika:

No, I wouldn't say that. To be completely honest, I've learned a lot more from their mistakes as real estate investors doing it all on their own than anything else because they just kind of went out there and did a lot of these things without having the knowledge that I have. Watching them do things through trial and error is why I sought out and invested for myself. I'm actually at a place in my life where I'm able to help my mom. She calls me for help on things with some of her deals, challenges, and other information that she needs regarding her land and properties. Now I can pitch ideas and solutions to her that we plan to put into action.

Shannon:

How does that feel?

Malaika:

It feels great. It feels good to know that I can help her and that's part of my main motivation for moving forward in my career. I know that things could be much better for her and could be more lucrative if she just had the knowledge and the resources and the skills that I have.

My reasons for being an investor and business owner are about more than just me and what I want. That was an evolution for me because initially my motivation was on the financial rewards. Now I realize that real estate is also a business where you can really help people and, for me, that starts with my loved ones.

Shannon:
What is the number one thing that you would recommend to someone who wants to get started in real estate investing?

Malaika:
I would recommend that they get an education. I think that's the number one thing all investors have to have. They have to seek the knowledge of how these strategies work, understanding the terms, knowing what's available, what to look for, how to avoid pitfalls.

There are lots of real estate investing programs available and lots of investors that teach various strategies. There are coaching programs available as well. There are a lot of popular books that we all know about, but they should begin to invest in themselves and their own knowledge. This is the first step that they have to take. They need to get a mentor, so it's not just reading the books or taking the classes. It's actually learning from the people that have been doing this for a long time who know what they're doing and to be able to have them as a resource and being able to tap their knowledge. For me that has been the critical element. Even with the knowledge, I don't think I would be a real estate investor if I didn't have mentors who I trust and are guiding me on this journey.

Shannon:
How has your education in real estate changed the way that you invest?

Malaika:
First of all, just getting the financial education, knowing how money works, and learning the tax code as it relates to real estate investing, has definitely been eye-opening for me. Then, learning from those that have been successful in this field but also when they shared their

mistakes, the things that they missed. That's important for me to know, and also, applying the knowledge. By working with a team of people I'm not just taking classes or reading books. I'm actually learning how to go out there and put those ideas into action and learn from them.

Shannon:

Do you have any favorite books that you've learned from?

Malaika:

Let's see, well, *Rich Dad, Poor Dad* is a favorite. I'm trying to think if there is another. It's not necessarily real estate related but it's business-related and that would be *The $100 Startup* by Chris Guillebeau.

It's a book where he interviewed entrepreneurs around the world about low cost startup businesses that they have. It is very inspirational to me to know that you don't have to have all the capital in the world to get started in a business. The same is true in real estate. If you have a dream and you have an idea, if you want to get started, there are ways to move forward with very little.

Shannon:

How is that?

Malaika:

There are a couple of ways, and I know that this is true for my mother because she's had her own financial challenges. She uses seller-financing. If there's a property that she's very interested in, then she can make an arrangement where the person who actually owns the home finances her. In a seller-finance, typically they would own it outright, and that could be an individual or it could be a company that's just been buying properties around the country.

Basically, they set up a mortgage with her without having to do things like running her credit or requiring her to have any capital. As long as she can make the arranged payments on time as it was laid out in that agreement, then it works for both parties.

Another option is wholesaling where, as an investor, you would be seeking properties that are for sale. It could be someone who's under distress, for example, who needs to sell because they're going through some situation. Let's say it's a divorce and they need to sell or it's a foreclosure or pre-foreclosure and they need to sell before those things accelerate, and you can negotiate with them, or the bank if it's a foreclosure, what their best selling price is.

After you get that negotiated price on your contract, you control that property even though you haven't purchased it. Since you aren't the end buyer you aren't going to have to put up the tens of thousands of dollars to purchase it, but you also have, within that agreement, the ability to assign it to an end buyer. They are the person with the capital. The person who has no capital may have to raise a nominal amount of money to have that property under contract. You can make a great deal off of that if you put in an assignment fee for yourself. Even just five to ten thousand dollars, depending on the value of the house, then you've made a great payday without having to use your own money or your own credit. If you are doing that once a month or more often, you earn a decent salary for yourself.

Shannon:
If you don't find a buyer by the time the contract expires, are you out that earnest money?

Malaika:
You could be, but it depends on how your contract is written. If it specifies that the earnest money deposit is non-refundable then you will lose that money. However, you could have a contract that has contingencies (for example: depending on inspections and partner approval) that allow you to get out before it expires and get your earnest money back. As the wholesaler, you can also require a non-refundable earnest money deposit from your end-buyer, which also minimizes risk. Some of the things that you learn in your education is to have contingencies in your purchasing contracts to minimize risk and to build your buyer's list ahead of time. You need to be communicating and building a team and have people who are looking for the properties that you'd be acquiring to wholesale so you have a list of people that you can market those properties to once you've gotten them under contract.

Shannon:

What are some of the processes that you should follow to be a successful wholesaler?

Malaika:

Finding and analyzing deals is a critical part of being a successful wholesaler. Many wholesalers damage their reputation from the outset by contacting potential buyers with deals that aren't deals in the first place. They haven't properly analyzed the numbers to ensure a profit for themselves and their end buyer.

Also, you would want to have a buyer's list so you want to know who's looking for properties and you want to know what their criteria is. Are they looking for three/ones or three/twos and what price range are they looking for? That's a first start, and I've heard from wholesalers who've been in trouble where they actually had a property under contract and they didn't have a buyer. One of the first steps is to go ahead and start talking to people and knowing what they're looking for first before you even actually start looking for properties. You want to know what the buyers want and then you maintain those relationships. Once you find a property that fits the criteria, you can share that information with them and let them know what their estimated repair costs would be and how much they would stand to earn in the end once the property is fixed and sold.

I've been looking at the real estate industry for some time, and I've purchased books from different people; the way that it's taught in many circles is a sort of "Wholesaling is so easy and you can make so much money in such a quick amount of time, thirty days to thirty thousand," or what have you, but learning from more knowledgeable people that I'm working with now, they let us know from the gate that this is simple in concept but not so simple to execute. This is actually one of the hardest strategies because you have to negotiate with both sellers and buyers. You have to know everything about the property. You've got to be able to satisfy the end goals between these two sides, in a way.

I know it's not an easy get rich quick. It's going to be some work. That is also why it is so important to have a mentor and people in place to help you get there. Even if you are educated in the technique and how it's done, the hardest thing sometimes is actually doing it. Taking that first step to initiate a potential transaction is easier said than done.

Shannon:
Does it still work to wholesale a home if somebody is upside down in it?

Malaika:
No, a wholesale wouldn't work in this case, but there are other options for investors to pursue. You could do a short sale, whereby you do a two-way simultaneous negotiation with the property owner and the bank (mortgage lender) so that the bank will accept less than what is owed on the property to avoid foreclosure or bankruptcy. Once the short sale is complete, you could sell the house for a profit in the near future or rent it out for cash flow. Short sales can be a great way for an investor to purchase a house at a reduced price; however, the process is usually lengthy (can take weeks or months) and, as with any real estate investing strategy, the investor still has to do their due diligence in regards to determining the condition and value of the home, costs for any repairs, any other associated costs, market analysis, etc., to ensure that it is a good deal and they will make a profit. Some investors avoid no equity or negative equity situations entirely while others are willing to pursue creative strategies depending on their knowledge and risk tolerance.

Shannon:
Why do you think it's important to have a single-person mentor versus only a formal education and books?

Malaika:
Oh, gosh, well just being able to build a relationship with someone that you trust, that's been incredibly valuable to me. I can call my mentor anytime. I can talk about the emotional roller coasters of starting a business, that kind of stuff with time management. We can bounce ideas off of each other. Also, if I have come across a property that may be good for a short sale or a wholesale deal, I can run that by him. I can give him the information. I can have him look at my

numbers and ask, "Does this make sense? Did I do this correctly and what strategy would you take?"

To be able to have someone be honest with you and say, "You know what? You didn't do enough here. You didn't give me enough information. You need to go back and ask these questions," Is priceless. A book or class can't talk back. A mentor also helps me in learning how to communicate with sellers, if I'm going to send a letter, if I'm going to make a phone call. What kind of questions should I ask? It is really valuable when you can have someone walk you through things rather than just doing everything on your own.

Shannon:
If you find a great house for $400,000 and you need to put $50,000 into it over three months, then your total price invested is $450,000. Is that accurate?

Malaika:
Not exactly, no. There's a lot more that goes into your costs when you're acquiring a property, and it also depends on your strategy. If you have $50,000 in repair costs over three months, you will also have costs associated with holding the property for the entire length of time to repair it. You'll have costs such as the utilities on the home, the taxes, the insurance on the home, and even when you buy and sell that home, there are costs associated with each of those transactions. This is if you flip it. If you keep it as a rental, or a buy and hold, you have to think about the vacancy rate in the area. You may have to set aside a certain amount of money in case you need to pay on a mortgage or the financing for the home while you get a tenant in place.

In both cases there are contingency factors since you never know until you start opening the wall or you start looking at the foundation; you just never know for a home that's been in a family for decades, or however long, what it really needs. Those repair costs may add $10,000 or more! You never know until you really get in there.

Shannon:
The unforeseen costs are unavoidable, but is there anything that would

make you walk away from a potential fix and flip?

Malaika:

It depends. The numbers have to work and you have to do your due diligence on the property. If the owner of the property or the bank are extremely difficult to work with, or are being unreasonable about the value, some people walk away because it is not worth their time and there are other deals out there. A lot depends on one's negotiating and communication skills. When working with sellers, you have to listen and figure out what they "actually" want. Most of the time it's more emotional than financial. You have to focus on solving their underlying problem.

Shannon:
How has real estate has changed your life?

Malaika:

It has been so eye-opening for me. If I hadn't taken a risk and taken action on getting educated and moving forward, I would have just done like so many people do: go to school, get a good job, work for forty years. All of this so you can pay bills and you die and you, hopefully, get a pension or a retirement plan and you hope that that works out. Now I've seen through personal experience and through being in the workforce that there is a better way.

I don't have to sit in a cubicle for eight hours a day if that's not what I want to do, and with my knowledge and the skills and the resources that I have now, I can create a much better retirement plan than any government or other entity could ever create. Also, just changing some of the ways that I used to think about money and some of the things that were taught about money, like the more popular money management philosophy: saving your way to wealth, staying out of debt, and focusing on saving. Instead there should be a focus on continuous cash flow where you're actually doing something to make money rather than just saving and hoarding it and hoping that it will be enough down the line.

Shannon:

What is cash flow?

Malaika:

Cash flow is your remaining income after your expenses, so whatever it is you're bringing in whether it be through a W-2 job or a business. Once you have that income and you've paid your bills, your living expenses, your fixed expenses, or your variable expenses, cash is what you have left over, and positive cash flow is obviously the thing that we all want.

Shannon:

Do you think that real estate is the best way to create that?

Malaika:

Oh, absolutely!

Shannon:

What is the difference is between massive income and passive income?

Malaika:

I've got a couple of examples of each. An example of massive income would be on a fix and flip. Let's just say you acquire a property and you know your repair costs and your holding costs, buying and selling costs, etc., but you've got such a great spread between those costs and your total after repair value. Let's say that spread is massive. Some people can make six figures on one fix and flip. That is massive income and that can happen if it's great and things go smoothly. It could be two to three months or maybe up to six months or longer if there were unexpected outcomes, but to me to be able to make a full six-figure salary essentially, when you compare that to what people make in a year, that is massive. Another example of massive income occurs from leverage. When you are able to build your business through the use of a team and systems, your income potential is unlimited. I think of that when I think of investors who are able to invest in multiple properties (single-family, multi-family, commercial, etc.) across the US because they don't have to physically be in those locations in order for things to run smoothly. They have teams and systems in place to monitor their investments.

On the passive income side, the best examples are rental properties. You may have to do some initial work on the front end, such as acquiring the property, making sure that it's fixed up, getting it rented, and establishing your property management, but all those things you can outsource to other people to do or help with. Then you are collecting rent from the renters and you aren't doing anything to make that money. You're not putting in sweat every day to make that money and you can just collect that while you go about your day-to-day life. That's what makes it passive.

Shannon:

In your real estate company, are you doing more fix and flips or more buy and hold?

Malaika:

Right now, I'm a money lender on a deal, so I was able to acquire enough capital to get my business started but also to help my mentor who's working on a fix and flip right now and contribute to some of the rehab costs; so I'm going to get a 10 percent return on that money that's been lent.

My initial strategy is I'd like to do some wholesale deals because I'd like to get in some relatively quick income from wholesaling. Then, I want to start with getting some massive income through fix and flips. After I've acquired a certain amount of capital, I will get into the buy and hold industry so that I have passive income coming in.

Capital needs to be set aside for some of those unseen costs; I want to make sure that I'm set really well before I get into the buy and hold strategies.

Shannon:

Where do you think you're going to invest?

Malaika:

I want to start with residential, with single family homes, and then work my way up to where I feel comfortable doing some commercial real estate investing. My mom owns a commercial building in South Carolina, so I'm communicating with her and my siblings on different things we could do with that space to generate consistent cash flow. We're discussing the needed renovations and marketing for a long-term lease agreement with an established business. It all depends on the market for that location, but I'd like to see her lease it to a franchise owner that has staying power. A well-established retail store, drug store, coffee shop, or restaurant would be nice.

Shannon:

Pricing on homes is a whole lot different than, say, your business partners in Dallas. Have you considered investing outside of California?

Malaika:

Oh, yeah. I see lots of opportunities in places like Texas as I see deals being posted in different real estate investing groups on Facebook and websites such as Craigslist. I could purchase multiple properties for the price of one here in Sacramento.

There are pros and cons to both. I definitely would love to be able to invest out of state and particularly in my home state of South Carolina. My mother already has property there. I want to help her make sure that those get cash flowing so that she has income coming in, but I would also want to build teams around the nation so that even though I can't physically be there, I would have people who would help build my real estate portfolio. They could take pictures of the property for me and help me with running the numbers and understanding what the market is like in that area.

Of course, I would still do my own due diligence as well. I would want to be able to travel to these places and put my own eyes and ears on the ground to know what's going on. That is a benefit that I see to having a team in different places. Also, being able to have passive income. Once it's all set up, once the places are fixed up, I'll hire property managers that are licensed and well-vetted and they can just maintain the property for me and send me the rent checks. That, to me, is a longer-term goal that I'm looking forward to.

Shannon:

Do you think it would be better to save the money and manage the properties yourself?

Malaika:

I don't. I've learned, especially recently, the value of my time, and time for me is becoming more and more valuable than money ever will be. So, to me, spending 10 percent out of what I make to go to property management and being able to live the life that I want to live, have more leisure time, be able to rest, and not be stressed out trying to manage and put out fires everywhere, is worth it

Shannon:

What type of legacy do you want to leave behind?

Malaika:

I've actually thought about this a lot because before I got into wanting to start a real estate business, one of the first things that so many self-help and self-development trainers tell you is that you have to have a 'why.' For me, it goes back to time. My time is so precious. I've spent most of my life in school and then I've been in the workforce, and I know that working forty hours a week for someone else is just not for me. I really want to live my life and enjoy my life. I want to spend time with my family, and so the legacy that I want to leave is one of freedom, really. Time freedom and financial freedom and sharing my knowledge and resources with other people so that they have that potential to be free too. That's ultimately my number one why.

Carl Volden &
Stac'ey Adams-Volden

Carl Volden has spent his professional career in software development working with startups, Fortune 500 Companies, and private
institutions across a variety of technologies and platforms that have
included many leadership opportunities. After the dot com bust, Carl
thought it wise to look for additional streams of income to provide for
his family.

Stac'ey Adams-Volden is an accomplished entrepreneur in her
own right, having worked with and for the likes of Howard Ruff,
Mark Stoddard, Michael Gerber, Stephen Covey, Bob Snyder, Jay
Abraham, Gary Halbert, Joe Girard, Robert Allen, Wright Thurston,
and Bryon Boothe. She has gone on to start and sell multiple businesses and assisted scores of others in helping them build and turn
their dreams into reality. She's owned an 800# service that took
orders for Mrs. Field's Cookies amongst others; started a book store
where she tripled the average book sales; marketed glow-in-the dark
dinosaur t-shirts that had 83 percent sell through in three days; been
a chef; owned a first-rate catering company; redesigned and sold a
children's series of workbooks that ended up being purchased by

Carson and Dellosa (the largest provider of supplemental educational products for educators and parents); and sold 60,000 units of a book to Sam's Club, to name a few of her entrepreneurial endeavors.

Together, Carl and Stac'ey have started a real estate business that has facilitated over $10,000,000 worth of real estate transactions as they provide solutions for distressed property owners and investor partners. And they've only just begun.

Contact Info:
OhanaPropertyVestors@gmail.com

Shannon:

How did you two know that you wanted to be involved in real estate investing? What inspired you?

Carl:

I don't know if it was any one thing that inspired me to get into real estate investing. It probably had more to do with life events than anything else. Shortly after Stac'ey and I married, we started talking about retirement and what we were going to do. I didn't have a 401K or any other retirement thing in place. Stac'ey had been self-employed for a number of years and didn't have anything either.

I recalled that while I was growing up, my Dad was involved in real estate investing. He did a number of fix and flips and he held some apartment units. We were involved as kids helping him fix those up. I thought, 'Well, there was an option." We looked into that and felt, "Yes, this is the path for us."

Stac'ey:

For me, I love helping people. I saw real estate as a vehicle to be able to continue doing that plus fund my retirement at the same time. I got married for the first time at forty. Previous to that I was married to my family and my work. I'd always put off retirement, investing, or even purchasing a home because that was something you did when you got married. Funny thinking, I know. However, now I was married, and, because of my age, I didn't have the luxury of a 401K blossoming into this mature, wonderful amount of money that I could retire on, so I had to look out around at what was available.

I'd been blessed to see the results of others' wise real estate purchases; plus, in my work, I had been exposed to all sorts of investing options. It came down to results that I thought I could replicate and wanted to be involved in. First hand I'd seen how my mother's home had appreciated through the years. Real estate was the investing vehicle that made sense to me. I thought, "Well, I simply need to go and find out how to do this and get it done."

Shannon:

How did you both decide how you were going to find out? Did you go down to the library?

Carl:

I went to a library, Stac'ey's library. My wife does a lot of reading and a lot of study and research, and in her library she has all kinds of courses. They came from previous employment experiences in her background and some from the different 'Gurus' that were around in that time frame. As I started looking through it, I soon realized most of them taught the same strategy, adding their own personal spin to it. Most unsettling though was when I learned none of these 'Gurus' were currently investing, and the information they were selling was the same content from when my Dad was investing decades before. I decided then and there that I wanted current information from real practitioners. I didn't want to make mistakes. I wanted to learn from the mistakes of others and not have to go down that road myself. I didn't feel like I had the resources to lose, so I was very cautious.

I think at that time I realized if we were going to move forward with real estate investing, I wanted to be educated thoroughly. Stac'ey and I then started our journey to find education that would work for us. It had to be hands on, taught by current successful real estate investors, and be information that would help us stay up-to-date with the ever-changing laws, trends, and market scenarios. Education we could see, feel, and learn from at our convenience while we were in the midst of family and work. Plus, we also wanted to have people around us who were doing the same thing so we could bounce things off of them. I'm the kind of guy that I didn't want it done for me but simply be there as a resource, to point me in the right direction, and help me see situations or problems I didn't see, as they share their experience and what it has taught them.

Shannon:

How can you earn money in a weak economy, and how can you earn money in real estate investing in a strong economy, and why do they differ?

Stac'ey:

You can earn money in both because there are different strategies to use. I like to use the metaphor of a tool belt. You have your tool belt and in your tool belt you have your hammers, your screwdrivers, your pliers, your wrenches, etc., and each tool has a specific job. It's hard to hit a nail with a screwdriver. It's hard to screw with a set of pliers. The tools are meant to do just what they were designed to do and nothing else. It's the same thing with real estate tools (strategies). You have to know which one to use and when.

If you try to use a Short Sale Strategy to acquire real estate in a good economy, it won't work as well because there's not much motivation for the home owner to work with you and there's also a lot more competition from other investors because there are fewer folks in trouble.

On the other hand, when the economy's down, that's what you do; you use a Short Sale. You help people out of foreclosure. Even though we knew some of this information, my husband and I found ourselves in an upside-down situation just the same: $100,000 in equity, doing a refinancing when the market turned, and we were now upside down.

The night before our home was to go to the Sheriff's sale, an investor came forward and bought it, but we didn't know there were any other options out there. We hadn't yet started our real estate education. We only knew a few things. The bank wasn't teaching us what our options were. We didn't see the mortgage companies coming forward and saying, "Well, you've got these seven options." We thought, "Well, okay, let's go out and get serious about this," and that's when we found a great educational company and started learning what those options were: what they meant to our credit, how to go forward, and how to educate others who found themselves in the same situation and what to do.

Come to find out, there were a lot of people in our situation. It's been wonderful to have this kind of education we've been able to get, and then be able to share those options with folks out there because nobody's teaching it. It's not something you read about in the paper. The articles and the headlines usually go something like, "35% of Homeowners are in Foreclosure" instead of "The 7 Different Solutions to Avoid Foreclosure," which is what we can now share. We go in and we help people. We educate them, because education is really where it's at. You get a foundation of good education, then you can make good decisions, but if you don't have all of the information that's available, you can't make a good decision. So, we go in and share the seven ways folks can solve their upside-down or in arrears situation.

A Short Sale is only one of the solutions in a list of seven that people can choose from. We guide them to what will be best for them in the short and long term and be the kindest to their credit report. It's hard, especially in today's credit world, to get back on your feet to purchase another home after a foreclosure. It's easier to get into a home after a bankruptcy than a foreclosure.

Shannon:
How do you find the people that are in trouble with their homes?

Carl:
When individuals find themselves in a foreclosure situation, there's been a Notice of Default (NOD) filed with the County Recorder. It's pretty much the same everywhere, whether it's a judicial state or a non-judicial state; some type of legal posting happens and it becomes a matter of public record. You can find them in the legal sections of newspapers, as they are legally required to be posted. If you have access to county land records online, you can access the same information there.

Also, there are title companies who will send you lists that have foreclosure information on it and you simply send mailers to these folks. Or you can go knock on their door and talk with them.

Shannon:
If you want to be a real estate investor, and you have little money or poor credit, what are some of the strategies that you can use to get into real estate?

Carl:
There's a couple I like because, you know, it doesn't take any money to do real estate investing. Well, I guess that's not quite true. It does

take money. It does take credit, but it doesn't have to be yours! With that said, Subject-To's, Seller Financing, and even Short Sales would be strategies I would look at getting into as a newbie, as somebody looking to get into real estate investing.

Even before that, I'd encourage somebody to invest in themselves. Get educated. Do their homework. Decide what kind of investing they want to be involved in as there are different kinds of strategies. I personally believe the more strategies you know and understand; the more effective you can be. It really comes down to what you know. Not everybody knows that you can use other people's money or other people's credit. Most everyone thinks they have to use their money, their credit and you don't.

Shannon:
What is a 'Subject-To'?

Carl:
A Subject-To is a strategy where the homeowner agrees to sell you their home subject to the existing mortgage staying in place. In other words, I'm going to go in and evaluate the property, find out they're behind say, two to three months. In order to bring them current, it's going to cost me say, $10,000. In return for me bringing their mortgage current, they sign their deed over to me. What happens there, I now have control of the property, but the mortgage stays in their name. I've effectively separated the mortgage from the property.

Shannon:
If they sign over the property to you, where do they go?

Carl:
Wherever they would like. We typically address that. Where would they like to live? How much do they need to get started? We can rent a U-Haul for them, if they've found a place they want to move in to; we can pay the first and last month's rent and deposit, whatever. It's all a matter of what their needs are and what can be reasonably done and still make sense. We negotiate.

As long as the numbers work out, and it's something they want to do, we educate them on what it is and what we want to do and how it works for them. Everything's up front and on the table. It has to work out for them too. It doesn't do me any good to try and create a deal, a Subject-To transaction, if they're not for it, if it's not going to work for them. The bigger picture is, we're building our business on the sound practices of respect and kindness instead of taking advantage of someone when they're in a vulnerable spot.

Stac'ey:
Right, because it's all about your reputation. It's all about the other person. That's what you're there for; to be a problem solver and an educator. Yes, we're not real estate investors; we're problem solvers and the more strategies we know, the more education we have; the more solutions we'll be able to come up with. My mom always taught me that she appreciated a good salesman because they educated her. I've always remembered that and thought to myself, "Well, that's what we are too." If we're going to be good real estate investors we're out there educating. We're educating people about their options. We're educating people about how to make the smartest decision for themselves.

And be yourself when dealing with people. If you drive a Mercedes, drive your Mercedes. If you drive a minivan, drive your minivan. I'm a minivan gal. You can't be something you're not. People can tell. They can smell it. It's all about trust. It's about developing relationships. This business is about relationships. It's a people business. You're a person and you're dealing with a person. We find each other in different seasons of our life and we have to be real and we have to offer real solutions. The more real education we have, the more real we can be.

They find, like we mentioned earlier, we can touch their hearts and share, "Hey, we've been where you're at and this is where you can go. You can make an average of $40,000 on a deal. You don't have to stay where you're at." I think when you're real like that and you're able to give people strategies and let them know that it doesn't take money or credit to do real estate, but it does require a good attitude and work ethic because everything else can be taught—you transfer hope from you to them. Income is a product of helping other people, but joy is the real income I think we find, and that comes from providing true help to folks who are in a needy situation, almost one of desperation.

Shannon:

Are a Subject-To and Seller Finance the same thing?

Carl:

There is a difference. With a Subject-To, the mortgage stays in the homeowners' name and the title is in the investors' name. The investor pays the mortgage and, if the investor misses a payment, as protection the home goes back to the homeowner. In the meantime, their credit is being built up with on-time mortgage payments. Typically, there's a date set when you as the investor buy the property and get it out of the homeowners' name.

On a Seller Finance, it sounds similar, however the difference comes in how you manage and distribute the equity in the home. As the buyer/investor, you make the payments to the seller on the agreed-upon terms. A great scenario for Seller Financing would be an older couple looking to sell. They want to move to a smaller, warmer town for example. They've lived in this home for a number of years, and they have an issue with capital gains if they receive all the money at one time.

By having them be the bank, you can get a little more creative with them in structuring how payments are made. Instead of getting all their money up front, putting them in the scenario of paying capital gains, you give them lump sums every year, skipping the need to go to the bank for financing. They're your bank.

Stac'ey:

You have more flexibility with Seller Financing and how to structure the payments; whereas, with the Subject-To's process, we simply leave the mortgage in place with all the terms the same and you take over the payments as is.

Carl:

I've brought them current, and in exchange for bringing the mortgage current, they sign their house title over to me, and I'll be the one continuing to make payments. That improves their credit, helps them out of a tough situation, and they can move on and start over. I typically rent out that property higher than what their mortgage is, thus providing me with cash flow. Everyone wins: the bank gets their mortgage on time, the former owner gets out of a tight spot, their credit improves with my on time payments, and I get a home using none of my own cash and a positive cash flow on top of it all.

Shannon:

Can you make improvements to the property since your name is now on the title?

Carl:

Yes, I can. With my name on the title, I control the property. The reality is I have no responsibility for the mortgage; however, if I don't make those mortgage payments, that house still gets foreclosed on because it's the mortgage that's being called. due. The bank claims the property. Even though I'm on the title, they still lay claim to the property.

Carl:

There was a comment or a question you asked earlier about investing in a down economy, and I love that question because I get it asked often: "How do you make money in a down economy?" My response is, "You can make money in any economy; up economy, down economy sideways economy, as long as you factor in cash flow." If you don't factor in cash flow, you're not going to make money. Every business, that's how they live—same with real estate.

It doesn't matter if the interest rate is 18 percent or 4 percent. If I can create a deal where the property will cash flow me positively after all expenses, I have cash flow and it's a deal. Regardless of what the interest is, regardless of if the economy is going up or down—if the numbers put me in a cash flow position, I'm in.

Shannon:
If a deal looks good on paper, but your gut is telling you there is some-thing wrong, do you do the deal or do you walk away?

Carl:
Go with my gut. If my gut says, "There's something not right here," and if I can't find it and anybody I share it with to help figure it out can't find it, I walk away.

Stac'ey:
I'd walk away. There are too many deals out there. There's a good deal every week. In fact, one of our teachers pounded into us that the deal of the decade comes around once a week. The thing that counts, Shannon, is that it's all about education. There's this one main thread that keeps coming back and that's the thread of educa-tion, because education saves you. It doesn't cost.

Education and community are what being a successful real estate investor is all about. Education gives you a firm foundation. In fact, to me, education is like the mighty oak tree. An oak tree drives its roots way down deep. It takes that deep foundation to hang on when people say, "Oh, you're stupid. You can't do this. Being a real estate investor isn't real work, go get a 'real' job." Because many of your family and friends around you, who want the best for you, will think and express sometimes that you've gone bonkers, but education will ground you and teach you what's right. There will be those who want to take advantage of you and say you need to do it this way or that but no matter what anybody says, or how hard they push you or how hard the winds of opposition blow, because you're based in current, solid, good education meaning the facts and the laws—you'll succeed because your roots go way down deep like the mighty oak.

Then in another way, you need to be like a redwood tree. Community is like the giant redwood tree. Did you know, a redwood tree can suck up to a thousand gallons of water every day? It can hold five hundred gallons of water in its trunk. Some of them were alive when Christ was here on earth. When one of those huge redwoods dies and falls to the ground, its fall is registered on the earthquake Richter scale.

Over 4,300 different types of plants and animals grow and thrive off of a fallen giant as it continues to give back. The roots of these redwoods grow out underneath the ground and grab on to the roots of the redwood next to it, and as they grow taller and taller, their roots grow out further and further and continue to grab on to and hang on to the roots of the other redwoods in the forest.

That's what our real estate community does. We hang on to each other, and we help each other grow and learn. When you have the deep educational foundation of the mighty oak and the root holding strength of the redwood-like community, there's no reason for you not to be wildly successful.

The other day I saw this really funny quote. Well, it wasn't so much funny as it was true: "You hang around five people who are intelligent, you're going to be the sixth; you hang around five people who are multi-millionaires, you're going to be sixth; you hang around five people who are idiots, you're going to be the sixth." It's who you hang around, so you have to be careful what you put in your head, and you have to be careful who you hang out with. Real estate investing gives you the freedom to do that–hang out with intelligent multi-millionaires and live the life you'd like to so you create the life you want.

We get to create for us, our older three boys and the two children we adopted from foster care. They were six and eight when they were born to us. They are now fifteen and seventeen. We believe that instead of buying our children all the things we never had, things that we'd always wanted our kids to have, I think it's more important to consider what we're teaching our children and that we teach our children all the things we were never taught. Material things wear out, but knowledge always stays with them, and being an example of that knowledge is what leaves the legacy.

Our children can watch us go out and get homes. They can watch us do real estate, and then no matter where they go in the country, they'll be able to have a home, and they'll be able to provide for themselves nicely. Not $15 or $20 an hour because that's not going to make it in today or tomorrow's world. Then if they want to become an artist, a singer, an inventor, a writer, or go to Africa and help build wells or build a school in Mexico or go do some other kind of needed service where their heart takes them, they can do that because they've got the funds. They can go to university and study what they want to, study what they find interesting, and not what will provide a living unless that's what they want to do because they'll have no money worries. They've got an income stream from their paid-off real estate investments. They'll have time to develop their talents and gifts and share them around. That to me is what real estate investing is all about. That's why we're passionate about it and that's why we're doing this.

Carl:

That's what real estate education is. It's investing in yourself and it will pay infinitely for an infinite return.

Shannon:

If you were to be a fly on the wall at your own funeral, what three things would you want people to say about you?

Carl:

I want to people to say, "He was a good man. Whenever I was around him, I felt loved and respected. He cared about me."

Stac'ey:

I want people to say, "She loved the Lord and He could always depend on her. I always felt loved and better about me and life by being around her. She saw the good in everyone and everything and life was fun."

With all of the challenges that Carl and I have gone through and have still to come, it's worth it because we can spend quality along with quantity time with our children and loved ones. We can live the life we create. We can go off and be of help when someone calls and asks us as we're not tied to the 9 to 5. When you're at the grocery store and you see a cute family standing in the next line over from you and you get this feeling that they could really use $100, you're able to reach into your wallet and quietly hand it to them. You know that's not much but it's a whole lot to them. A hundred dollars still means a lot to us, and then you get to give your children quite a legacy of love and learning and freedom.

Carl:

It's a grand life, and real estate helps us to make it even grander, because 52 percent of American's have less than $1,000 in savings and how are they going to get out of the rat race? They've got to do something different. It requires us to change, and we have to stop trying to work our way out of the hole. We've got to generate income, and we've got to generate wealth, and it can't be something we're physically tied to doing. We've got to be able to change the dynamics of how much we're taxed in relation to how much we're earning. We've got to acquire these assets that make money for us. This is urgent for everyone.

Carl & Stac'ey:

We go by this adage:

Stick to your task till it sticks to you.
Beginners are many; enders are few.
Honor, power, place and praise,
Will always come to the one who stays.
So, stick to your task, till it sticks to you.
Bend at it, sweat at it, smile at it too.
For out of the bend and the sweat and the smile,
Will come life's victories after a while.

JC & Linda Williams

Linda Williams attended the University of Redlands, California and the University of Arizona, in Tucson, where she majored in Commercial Advertising with a Fine Arts Degree. She minored in Music, playing the harp. After spending nearly 35 years in advertising and marketing, she had the opportunity to change careers, after being laid-off after 19 years with the company. She currently resides in Tucson, Arizona, with her husband JC Williams where, as an entrepreneur, she runs a successful real estate investing firm. She is adamant about never going back into corporate America. She is always looking for win-win situations which complement her relationship-based personality. She feels that having the time to spend on her relationship with her husband and family could only happen because she is no longer spending 10-12 hours a day working for someone else.

JC Williams attended the University of Phoenix as a triple major undergrad (Administration, Management, and Marketing) and completed his MBA in 2003, after spending many years as a computer consultant and systems analyst. He also taught at University of Phoenix in 2005 and 2006. In the mid-eighties, he spent some time investing in Tax Liens. The year of 2007 brought about many changes, including the desire to get back into investing. He currently resides in Tucson, Arizona. He and his wife run a real estate investing business which allowed them to leave corporate America in 2011. He is always looking for opportunities to help others with both their financial freedom and to solve their real estate related dilemmas.

Contact Info:

JC and Linda Williams

jcwilliams@osodeloro.com

lkwilliams@osodeloro.com

www.osodeloro.com

Shannon:

According to Forbes magazine, real estate investing is one of the best ways to create wealth. Do you agree with that statement?

Linda:

Yes, I do. I have been in another career for years and this was something that I'd always wanted to do, and we've been doing it for 9 years. Totally agree, we are out of the corporate world now.

Shannon:

What about you, JC?

JC:

Personally, I absolutely believe that real estate is the answer to long term deep wealth. If you manage your properties and related investments well, you can never run out of money. You can if you are in other investment arenas. I just don't think that for developing deep wealth that there's anything other than real estate to do that in.

Shannon:

You know, it's interesting that you say that "if you manage your properties and related investments well..." What do you think the difference was between those people who lost everything in 2008, and the people who didn't?

JC:

I think the primary difference is there were people who called themselves investors, who were not really investors. When the economy was so overheated, where the person down the street, that was a hairdresser, was buying a house at full retail, throwing more money into it, and was able to sell it, and make a profit, that's not investing. That is just taking advantage of a current situation. Those are short lived bubbles, those really are. An investor is a person who goes out, finds a piece of property that they know when they're going into the property, they're going to make a profit; either long term profits by having it as a buy-and-hold, or it's going to be short term profits because they're going to wholesale it, or they're going to repair it and then sell the property back out into the market as a flip. A lot of people were trying to do flips. Those people that I know that were actually investors, they didn't go out and pull every bit of cash out of their properties and become actually upside down on their income model. You can't be in a situation where you have alligators chewing on you every single month and expect to live, if your job goes away or something else happens.

A true investor, in my mind, makes sure that all of their properties, in a buy-and-hold, are always in a positive cash flow situation. If it is a negative, that it is such a slight negative that all of their other properties will take care of it without it becoming a burden, where they have to pull money out of their pocket through a job or some other source of income in order to manage and maintain that particular property.

Shannon:
How did you get started in Real Estate?

JC:
Actually, we got started because we were afraid of never being able to retire. We ran across a chart about 10 years ago that showed that we would need $3.4 million dollars in order to retire for 25 years, taking out $10,000 a month. The problem was that we only had a couple hundred thousand dollars in our 401(k)s and our 403(b)s. Being 14 years away from retirement age, at that magical 65 years old, there was no way that we could see that we were going to be able to retire.

At a friend of mine's birthday party, a year later, I ran into a guy that asked me very simply, if I felt that, without really thinking hard about it, if I could find a property, here in Tucson, that would give me something like $500 a month in cash flow? I had to admit that, yes, it was possible. I had written some software for a property management firm and I saw what the owners of those properties were taking home every single month. Yeah, it was possible. As he said, "Well you know, $500 a month isn't going to retire anyone, but if you could find 1, could you find another 9, let's say over the next 3, 5, 7, 10, whatever number of years that you need to do that?"

I said, "Well, yeah, it's kind of like a step and repeat." He says, "Well, if you have 10, that's $60,000 a year that's coming in the door that you're not working for, that there are other people who work all month in order to make sure that you're one of the first people that they pay every month." I said, "Okay wise guy, so that's all fine and dandy, I need like 20, how do I do this?" He says, "Sounds to me like you need some serious real estate investing education." He introduced us to some education and we started down that road and believe it or not, it took 3 and a half years to leave corporate America. We started in June of 2007, and by February 1, 2011, we were no longer involved in corporate America, and haven't been for over 5 years. That is a thing that has changed our lives, and that's how I got started in real estate investing.

Linda:
I had worked a corporate job for over 30 years. I thought I was secure for what I was doing and that I would eventually retire from that corporate job and have real estate investing on the side. Like many corporations in the United States, I was laid off from my last job after 19 years, that's been 7 years now.

Like many Americans, I thought I was secure with what I was doing and what I had learned to do as a career, and real estate investing was going to be a side venture for us. I have several real estate agent friends who also invest. However, they wanted me to become an agent like them, but I was not interested in selling properties as a profession. When the layoffs occurred, I realized how fortunate I was that I had learned how to do this. We'd gone through about 2 years of applying our investing education, we've been in and realized that I would be able to go forth, not have to move from Tucson, like some of my corporate associates had to. I wanted to stay here because it's such a great market and our home. I was actually able to stay here doing real estate investing full time. I was somewhat thrown into it but loved the fact that I enjoyed it and that we would be able to retire eventually. Whereas my other job, I did not think I would be able to retire like JC said.

Shannon:

Linda, in your opinion, what is the number one mistake an individual makes when buying their first investment property?

Linda:

I feel that the number one mistake is that they don't know to have multiple exit strategies in case something goes wrong.

Shannon:

JC, do you agree with that being the number one mistake?

JC:

I think the number one mistake is that they want it so bad that they will ignore some of the warning signs. I've seen this too many times. I helped people that have, they jumped into a deal that they got emotionally involved in, instead of being strictly by the numbers. I think that's probably the number one thing that you learn over time, is that you temper your, I call it your enthusiasm. You temper your enthusiasm, because a lot of people want that first deal. When the deal doesn't work out, they get so disappointed. The bottom line is that they're looking too much at the short term and not the long term.

I know I've been talking with people these last couple of weeks about what I call the long game. The long game is if I acquired this piece of property, where am I going to be sitting with this property 3 years from now, 5 years from now, 10 years from now, 20 years from now, whatever the time frame is, that's the long game. If that property does not make sense in your strategy, and that's one of the things that you need to come up with is a hard strategy that says this is what I need to have in that piece of property, then don't do it. If it doesn't fit, you have to let the emotions go and just say, "It doesn't fit." Whether it's your first property, or if it's your fiftieth property.

I'm right now working on putting together a very large portfolio. It's millions of dollars' worth of properties. You can get caught up very quickly in an emotional state where you want it so badly that you ignore the warning sign. You always have to rein yourself back in a bit and make sure the numbers fit, first and foremost. I think that's the number one thing that people, their first deal, their first couple of deals, is getting the emotions out of the way, just letting it be strictly by the numbers.

Linda:

Shannon, another thing that's very critical in my view is the education that we work with is always updated to what the laws are now. The laws are changing dramatically from when we started to today. The classes are always being redone to update what's going on in the United States and the rules and regulations on investors. One thing that we encourage students to do is always, always, always update themselves on the current information that is out there, so they also stay within the parameters of their state and what's going on. It's rather easy because the education is always taking care of that, on a national level.

Shannon:

What is the difference between bird-dogging and wholesaling?

JC:

The major difference between bird-dogging and wholesaling is whether or not the person is on the title. In bird-dogging, a person has no legal interest in the piece of property, in any way, shape, form, or fashion. They don't have a contract in place. They don't have anything, there's nothing there. Now, if they took an option on the piece of property, or they have a contract that they're now in escrow with, then they have a legal interest and they are not bird-dogging. Those are situations where a person is already involved. They could maybe be the financial partner to somebody else. They're doing the financing on a piece of property, and they want to roll out of their particular position. There's different things as far as how you are actually directly involved with that piece of property. If they sell the property to someone else, after they take possession, without fixing the property, then that is a wholesale.

A bird-dog is a person that has no direct interest in that piece of property. They may say something to an investor like, "Well I heard that Joe Schmo has this piece of property, I went over, I took a look at it, looks like something that you may be interested in." They hand the information off for a fee to somebody else. That other person actually then contacts Joe Schmo, does the actual transaction, and completes it. That is a bird-dog situation. By the way, Bird-dogging is currently illegal in Arizona.

Shannon:

Is wholesaling legal in Arizona?

JC:

Wholesaling always is legal, because you always have a legal interest in that piece of property. Another option is assigning your position.

Let's say I took an option out on a piece of property. In other words, I have contracted with the owner of that property to purchase it by a specific date in the future at a particular price, I could sell that option. Totally legal, because I have a legal interest in that piece of property. I could sell that option off. Now, if I am under contract, I just opened escrow today on a piece of property and I want to get rid of that piece of property, and I don't want to close on it.; I have an option: I can assign it, which is a really easy way of doing it, and that is just a piece of paper where you go ahead and you assign your interest in that piece of property to somebody else. It's a legal document, and I extract a fee for doing that.

Let's say that you're in line to buy tickets to a Taylor Swift concert. You have a particular position there. Then somebody comes up and says, "Hey, I would like to give you $100 to have your place in line." That's an assignment. You had a legal position. You were legally in line, right? You didn't take cuts. Somebody's buying your position. That happens all the time.

Shannon:

Explain to me why a real estate investor would use tax liens as an investment strategy.

JC:

For me, I've done tax liens. There's two sides, actually. It's a great place to park money Like here in Arizona we have a great interest rate on tax liens, it's a 16% per annum simple if you're buying it over the counter. The other side is the opportunity to acquire the property itself. If you're buying the tax lien at the auction, you may end up bidding down the interest rate that you're willing to take. I don't personally do the auctions because there's a lot of stupid people that bid down the interest rate, down to something that is unreasonable. I consider it a horrible death for your money because you can't make good returns on your money at 2, 3, or 4%.

I've had people actually bid the lien down to those types of interest rates. The problem that you have: not every property that you get a lien on are you going to get the property. In fact, in my experience, it's been a very small percentage of the properties that I have tax liens that I actually acquired the property. It is at this point I would say somewhere in the neighborhood of 3, 4%. If the majority of the time, you're not going to get the property, then you need to look at it from the point of view of what is your money doing. Now, 16% per annum simple is a great place to park your money. You will have the opportunity to foreclose on their right to redeem their back taxes and one of two things are going to happen. They can pay off their taxes and pay off the lien and now it is cleared. They don't have to worry about somebody coming in and foreclosing on them. They may have more than one lien out there for different years, and that's a whole different story. The second is that they do not respond and we end up foreclosing and receive the property.

The bottom line is, is that if I am looking at a return on investment, because I'm an investor, I don't look at the fact that I will get that piece of property. I have to look at the worst case scenario in all situations. Worst case scenario is I'm making just money on my money. If I don't acquire that piece of property, is 16% return on investment a good return? Well, yeah, right? Also, if the property is being sold, back taxes are generally caught up.

In the second scenario you actually have to go through the foreclosure. Typically, when you initially send in the letter with intent to foreclose on their right to redeem, it shakes them up and they go down, they pay, and now you're going to get a check from the county for your initial investment plus the interest that these people are paying. That's good. If you do go through that entire process and you acquire the property, is the property worth the dollars? Obviously, liens are down in the neighborhood of 10% or less of the assessed value of the property because it's based upon the taxes that are due on the property. Rarely, you have 100% tax on a property. Only in rare cases (20 or more years of back taxes due) do you have a lien that is equal to or greater than the value of the property as the taxes are never what the property's actually worth.

I always look at it from the first point of view as that is what I'm going to be receiving as money from money. That's the way I see it. That's why I say going down 2, 3, 4, or 5% is stupid because more than likely, that's what you're going to get. You're not going to get the property.

Different states have different rules and if you don't understand the rules, then you're going to set yourself up for trouble. That's where education comes in huge.

Shannon:
Have you had any specific mentors in your real estate investing that have helped you navigate potential pitfalls?

JC:
I ran into a situation where I bought a piece of property that I chased. That's where you learn about the emotional side, okay? I chased this property, I ended up buying it for $68,000. I needed to really buy it for $60,000 because that $8,000 would have actually done the rehab, and then I could've sold it.

I called one of my instructors and I said, "Hey, I'm in this situation, what do you think I should do?" When the instructor said, "Well, how much is the property actually worth?" I said, "I think it's worth about $100,000." The instructor said, "You think or you know?" I said, "No, I think, that's what all the numbers say." He said, "Okay, why don't you do this, why don't you spend a couple hundred bucks, get yourself an appraisal for the after repair value, and then sell it based upon that knowledge?" I did. He said, "Okay, what you need to do, you need to put an ad in Craigslist that says, handyman special, then go about it that way." I was just waiting to be able to close on the deal, what I did is that the day that we closed, I put an ad out in Craigslist. This was on a Thursday, I put an ad out on Craigslist that said, "Handyman special, you fix, you profit." Then in the body of it, it said, "Property fresh appraisal, $104,000 after repair, owner willing to let it go for $75,000, $5,000 down owner will carry."

I showed the property on Friday. I showed the property on Saturday, on Sunday, and we actually sold it and closed on it on Monday.

Having people that have the knowledge and have the experience, they have been down the road that you are going down. They can give you that type of knowledge. They can give you those hints and those abilities. That's what a valuable coach can give you. Dana was one of my coaches. I've also had, Jeff Armstrong, who is the number two seller financed note buyer in the United States. He's become a very good friend of mine. He's the one who said, "Hey, why don't you just sell it and carry the paper?" I said, "Okay."

The end result is that I think the last time I looked, we still have that property, well, we don't have the property, we have the note. This is, I think 6 years later, we have made over $40,000 in profit so far, and they still owe us another 60 plus thousand dollars on the note. Even if they went out tomorrow and they were to refinance and pay us off, we'll make well over $100,000 on this piece of property just because we had the opportunity to talk to somebody who is knowledgeable and who's able to give us some ideas of ways to go. He was actually more interested in helping us than you know, "Pay me something and I'll tell you." It was strictly, "Hey this is the way I would do it."

Linda:

That opened the door to continuing calling on these practitioner instructors, people that are more experienced or have gone through different experiences in their real estate investing arena, so we can ask them their opinion, which is what we value from this real estate investment education. Everyone is out to assist others and get opinions about what they're doing, and we know we'll get an honest, straight forward answer from them.

That's why 9 years of experience has attributed to our ability to advise others.

The peaks and valleys we've been through, and we're very much people of integrity and honesty, and we want the best for everybody that we work with. We're very tuned in. That's my goal in life is to assist many people, to help them get their financial freedom that they deserve in this lifetime.

Shannon:
What do you want people to remember about you? What is your legacy?

JC:
I think probably the first thing I want people to say is that I was always straight with them. I never gave them any moments that they needed to doubt my word, or I call it my veracity. The second is that I was genuinely concerned about people and where they were heading in their life and how I could positively affect their lives. Whether they took it or not, it didn't make any difference whether they actually did anything that we had talked about it, but that I was genuinely concerned about who they are, where they're going in their life, and how they're going to get there. The 3rd thing that I was a great advisor, that I was a great example to them of what was possible, that I gave them not only my knowledge, I also gave them my time and my direct concern for them.

Linda:
That people knew I cared about them and that they meant the world to me. At the end of the day relationships are all we have. We do this business because we want to strengthen and lift people which only builds lasting relationships. As a couple, this opportunity to be real estate investors and advisors to others looking for a different financial platform to build their lives upon, has been a great journey that has given us the ability to both strengthen our relationship, and others.

Atarah Wright

Atarah Wright is a Wealth Educator for ParentPreneurs. She is the creator of Wealth First Financial Education products, services and events to guide families to saving time & money, increase cashflow, spend more quality time with family & friends while building a lasting legacy for generations to come, having fun and doing it with love. She is a published author, a transformational speaker and coach who inspires action.

Her work began when she gained her own financial plan, implemented it, and then became a financial services representative and real estate investor back in 2001. She turned her wealth of knowledge into sharing strategies to allow more people to build wealth and prosperity. She invites you to join the wealth first movement on Facebook to learn, implement and grow with her. She is the wife of Jimel L. Wright for nineteen years they are proud to have four beautiful children together.

Contact Info:
Atarah Wright, Wealth Educator, Transformation Speaker/Author/ Coach/Real Estate Expert • CEO of Atarah Wright Consulting Firm
www.atarahwright.com • www.wealthfirstmovement.com
Atarah@AtarahWright.com • Twitter: https://twitter.com/msatarah
Facebook: www.facebook.com/groups/wealthfirstmovement
LinkedIn: https://www.linkedin.com/in/atarahwright

Shannon:

What inspired you to get involved in real estate investing?

Atarah:

Honestly, I was drawn to real estate investing because I saw so many different types of people making money in so many different types of ways. I am so amazed to be in this space and producing good work. I know it is all because I became committed to financial education and becoming a real estate investor.

I know one thing for sure, financial knowledge was given to me as a gift because, as I have become confident in my investing abilities, I share with others and help them understand how real estate investing has so many various investing styles. Any one of them can build long-term wealth for generations to come.

Shannon:

How has your education changed the way you invest in real estate?

Atarah:

When I decided to take action with my husband on board, we met many other investors who poured into us their knowledge, tips, tricks and how they learned from their own mistakes. When they saw how young we were, getting started in our early twenties, they were impressed and wanted to see us succeed. Sometimes, I wonder if they wanted to see us succeed more than we did. We were in a vicious cycle of learning. We learned so much we were paralyzed by all of the opinions we were hearing. Being young it became hard to decipher fact from opinion.

I was confused why, if real estate investing was a legitimate way to get rich, people were not willing to take the risk. They were raising their families, trying to get by paycheck to paycheck, barely making ends meet. Why did they still feel a "job" was the only way to live?

It didn't take long for us to know having a "job" was like putting all of your eggs in one basket. I wanted to scream from the top of the mountains: "Over here! Yes, over here! I found a better way and you don't have to quit your job! You can use your w-2 income, no matter how much you have, to get started in real estate investing and building wealth for your family!"

I know God is using me, helping me speak up and speak out so those who will hear will be blessed with an array of knowledge, all because I decided to go against the grain. It's truly amazing.

Shannon:

Did you do it? Did you stand on the mountain top and scream?

Atarah:

It's funny you ask. In reality, I would have if I had been given the chance, and in a metaphorical way, I did. I believe people look at me and say, "If she can do it, I can do it. Maybe she can help me. Maybe she knows someone who can help me."

The nice thing is, I know I can help. I have been tasked with financially educating a certain group of people who just don't know. I accept the mission and work daily to walk in my greatness. Although I still have a lot of room to grow on my personal journey, I know my upbringing helped me to be a better, stronger person so I can inspire others to take action and figure it out. It's simple, but not easy. I have been given seeds which were planted over my lifetime.

The seeds have grown in to a deep knowledge of the science and understanding of how wealth is built. My inspiration is my parents. I never knew until I dug deeper. I took my upbringing for granted. I realize now they were teaching and planting seeds my entire youth, but they didn't even know they were doing it.

My journey and the phenomenal changes have been manifested in my life, even in the last year, are nothing short of miraculous.

Shannon:

According to Forbes Magazine, real estate is one of the top three ways to create wealth. As a real estate investing expert, why do you feel this is the case?

Atarah:

Real estate investing is one way to create wealth. Starting a business filling a need is another way to create wealth. By owning your own business, you can build passive income. Once you set the business up and add a powerful team, you can enjoy life a little more. I feel strongly a third way to build and retain wealth is to have precious metals like gold and silver coins. Metals also respond to specific market conditions and are closely valued with the movement of the dollar. The value of precious metals increases when the dollar is weak and value decreases when the dollar is strong. I've learned when you build wealth as you pursue your passion you will have more success. I just happen to be passionate about a lot of things including real estate, and real estate is the number one way over all of them. It's number one although it's cyclical people will always need a roof over their head so it is profitable for real estate investors whether it's a good or bad market. Investing in real estate is not as risky, nor does it take a lot of time and the cash on cash return is phenomenal.

Shannon:
What is bird dogging?

Atarah:
Bird dogging is where you find a deal and you bring it to the wholesaler or person who wants to buy and hold it; so you bring it to an investor who has the capital or the education and they give you a fee of $500 to $2000 for finding it for them. You look for the property not listed on the MLS, and you share it with a wholesaler who then will get it under contract, and then find an investor who wants to buy and hold it or fix and flip it. It is a good way to start earning money with little or no risk.

Shannon:
What is wholesaling?

Atarah:
Wholesaling is when you find the property and get it under contract to sell. The owners may have a foreclosure, or they're going through a divorce, or they're in need to do a short sale, and they take the property and they say, "Hey, fixer flipper, I have a friend," or, "I met someone who has a property and you may want to talk to them, here are the numbers." The wholesaler is taking the time to do a quick evaluation

of the deal using an actual formula, and it's an evaluation of how much money I can make and how much money I can flip this contract for. You want to be a knowledgeable, educated wholesaler. Wholesaling and birddogging are different because a wholesaler actually goes into contract on the property a birddog does not. When you're wholesaling, you can get paid on average $5000 by finding a deal.

Once they're in contract, that's how you get paid. When they sell it to 'ABC' buyer, who has the cash or the loan, once they close the wholesaler receives the $5000, or if the wholesaler's good like I am, then they can get paid the money up front and not actually have to pay the closing fee. Wholesaling is owning the rights to buy or sell the property. I've made as much as $22,000 on one wholesale deal. However, I made sure there was enough room for the homebuyer to actually have equity so it was a win-win. Wholesaling is a great way to build up cash to fix and flip and eventually become a landlord buying and holding. I recommend an investor start here; it's less risky.

Shannon:
With wholesaling, do you ever actually own the property?

Atarah:
You own the right to buy or sell the property. You own the contract. Then you market that contract to investors or homebuyers who like the deal. You can get really creative with real estate investing.

Shannon:
Do you have a favorite mastermind group or network?

Atarah:
Yes, I'm a proud member of several masterminds. I found these masterminds and study groups through Renatus. Inside this community I learned about one of my mentor's ups and downs in real estate and his mistakes and successes while building his business, his story really blessed me. When you think about real estate, it's a tool, just like money. It has no power other than what we give it; if we are tapped into ourselves, our space, and our emotions, we can give it more power. The better we

get at understanding the power we have to manifest using the wealth-building tools, the better and more sustainable our lives become. We have to understand we are the master of the money. The money is not the master of us telling us what we can and cannot do. Money is just a tool to build wealth. It's phenomenal.

I'd also like to add another reason building relationships is highly important is because I've learned how to raise private money from private investors.

Private money is money that's not received traditionally, like through a bank or a loan broker. It's someone who has a retirement account looking for a better return on their money. They're out here searching and they're going to invest, so they may like you and your deal. You find out what they want through relationships, you find yourself networking with these people, ask the right questions to see if they like the deal. I actually learned a lot of whether a private money investor will invest with you or not, is based upon your own knowledge and the ability to show them how they will make money.

I was surprised it is not as hard as one might think. People believe in you when you believe in yourself. I highly recommend reading How to Win Friends and Influence People. We should all study it because it helps us become better people. That's what I love about that book. It's not just, "Oh, well I just need to know how to get friends and then I'll have everything I want." No, you've got to learn how to be a better person so you attract the type of people and then you'll influence them and they'll influence you. I definitely use it as a tool to help me be in any space where I can. If I can offer to help, even if it's a little thing since I don't have a lot of time, I will. It is a part of who I am. Collaboration in its purest form. Together, we can do anything. Masterminding is truly an asset.

Shannon:
How has real estate Investing changed your life?

Atarah:
Real estate has done so much for me, especially the financial educational part and the personal development. I'm a preacher's kid and

my mother had me when she was two months from being seventeen. My mother, Eva Farr Wallace, and my biological father, Calvin Jamison, got married very young. They had a short marriage. She moved on, and my late father who raised me, Bishop Otis Pete Dawson, inspired all of this. He is no longer with us; he passed away March 26th, 2004. My mother helped him to find out how to live his dream. She had some challenges to overcome, and she faced them with the power of God and just pure will to win, and when she failed she learned from it and got back up and did it again. She still motivates me today. I'm so proud of her.

Here I was at five years old watching my father, who didn't even own a home. I didn't know anything about this, so when I assess my education now, I see what this little girl was witnessing. I was just a child playing, being a kid. However, they were planting seeds in my life which are manifesting in me today.

My mother had a job, my dad had a job, and he wanted to build a church.

These seeds are being dropped; this example is in front of me for life.

They had a restaurant, they did build a church, and they also built their home on the same land.

After my dad passed, my mother did not want to continue to keep the church, she wanted to move on, so she did a lease option. This is all without the formal education of how this process works. She thought, "This is how I'm going to do it." And she figured it out.

I don't have all the details of her thoughts and dreams; I can just assess what I witnessed and how it affected my actions. She did the best she knew how, and when she could get help she took it. Rather than waiting 'til the building was built and they raised the money, we started the church in our home, in an apartment. We opened the doors. It was me, my little brother, my mom and dad. We were sitting in an apartment creating a dream. No one sat us down and said, "This is how you make your life and create your life." We weren't just told the impossible could happen. We watched the impossible become possible. My brother has also passed away, Sergeant Ezra Dawson, on January 17th, 2009. I lost both of them in physical form. However, their memory carries on.

People came. They came inside our apartment and they prayed with us, they sang, testified, and studied the word of God. They joined my dad, and he began to build his church. My mother began to look for the money. We became entrepreneurs. We sold dinners. We used to get inside of the trash cans so we could get cans and turn them into cash to use for what we needed, funds to build the church. It was nothing because we were kids and kids love being messy. I have come long way on this journey. I continue to walk in my purpose figuring it out along the way.

My mother was a government employee. She worked for the IRS. She delved into every part of it. She used to teach classes every tax season. They would actually have her travel to San Antonio and Houston. Sometimes we traveled with her during the summer. She would stand and teach hundreds of people the tax law. I take a lot of my strength from my mother.

On December 31st 2015, I decided to get coaching to write my own book, Wealth First: Stop Stressing and Start Manifesting, to help inspire people to focus on the solutions to fixing your stressful problems instead of wallowing in pity about how you messed up. The sooner a person can start focusing on their option to minimize stress, the sooner they can have relief. They should be focusing on manifesting and not procrastinating. We should also take our time to think through any issues that might come up. I learned this through trial and error.

I'm excited to know one day my children will be adults and have a better understanding of what their dad and I had to go through. As a little girl I adored seeing her outside of the church in what we called "worldly space." We were non-denominational Holiness is what my dad taught. His work with church people, saints of God, teaching God's word pure and raw. My mother was a network marketing queen. She was in Amway, Avon, everything. She is now my business partner behind the scenes. So we get to work together today. As a child, I saw her in those company overview meetings, she would take me along. She would have me participate too. We were always being taught ways to make a particular business work. I learned from my parents to be a servant leader and simply being of service where you can. If you have time; donate an hour, a day, or a week of your life to helping someone less fortunate than you. It's just good manners.

My dad used to say, "I don't care what kind of education you get, where you go in life, if you don't have good manners, it's the worst kind of person to be rude and unkind when we have so much to be grateful about." My parents taught us to be humble and grateful for everything. You want to be liked, you want to be loved, you want to be cared about. Be human. Treat people like you want to be treated.

We can study the pathways of people like Bill Gates and Warren Buffet and go back twenty years and see what they were doing. At thirty, forty or fifty, where did they go to school? What did they learn? How were their mannerisms? How do they appear to us in media? Are they firm? Are they strong? These are lessons I want to teach people, because it's truly a wealthy mindset.

Shannon:
What advice would you give to someone who is allowing fear to hold them back from starting real estate investing?

Atarah:
Do it afraid. Walk right up to it and say, "I'm going to do it anyway," and then get the education you need to give you the confidence to take another step, and another step. Get the support, invest in yourself, find a mentor, join one of my group masterminds. I have an audio on my website that I'm giving away which teaches you to manifest anything you want. You must decide. Commit, and then become an excuse eliminator by becoming your own superhero. So when excuses come up you put your superhero cape on and knock them out of the park. Real estate is a cyclical investment so you need sound advice from people of all walks of life who have the experience to help you keep going until you win and achieve the results you want. I'm in a real estate investment education organization that teaches real estate investing; however, when I invite someone to become a part of our real estate investment organization, I want them to know it is going to also be personal development, too.

Shannon:
You have talked repeatedly about your parents being great mentors and

great examples to you. How important do you think it is to have a mentor that is actually in real estate investing and why?

Atarah:

A mentor who has done it and learned the lesson is very important. They help you shorten your learning curve. It gives you accountability. Mentorship can be gained from an actual live person communicating with you or you can get mentorship from the educators teaching real estate investing. The current mentorship I have in real estate investing came to me through my wonderful husband Jimel Wright. I've been awarded an opportunity to have a multi-millionaire teach me more about multiplexes and commercial real estate investing. He is currently walking me through how to assess a Performa and create a marketing package to take to venture capitalists. When you build the right relationships and stay aligned with your purpose, you can attract the right mentorship along the way. There are a lot of other mentors I have in my real estate investing education organization. I joined the community to have access to a support system, so if anyone is looking I would say look no further.

Shannon:

Why is passive income important?

Atarah:

Passive income is your money working harder than you have to work for it. You can get passive income from a rental property. You invested in the property, fixed it up, rented out to help a family who needs a place to live, they pay you which pays the mortgage. You earn a net profit after expenses are paid for which is passive income. Now that's sweet. Passive income is important because it allows you to have different income sources other than your job. You see, nowadays, there is no job security. The 40-40 retirement plan is extinct. We are taught to go to school, get a good education, then work hard and you will be successful. Unfortunately, it is not working. Passive income, if setup right, allows you to receive income from your investment properties or businesses. When something happens to your job you are not completely out of income.

Passive income allows you to have more freedom and creates a better quality of life; it reduces stress, if I do say so myself.

Every one of us should be investing in one property a year. It will create a nice retirement fund and reduce taxes. If you have the right education, passive income can save you money, save you time by not stressing over the loss of a job due to unforeseen circumstances. Passive income can help you have money for your children's college. Passive income helps create freedom so you can create your own wealthy life-style. Passive income creates freedom.

Shannon:
What is your legacy that you want to leave behind?

Atarah:
I am a wealth educator which allows more control over my time. It's great, to have the option to attend meetings all week; however, I have four beautiful children, so when the opportunity allows, I take them on the journey with me like my parents did.

I dream of saying to them, "We're going to be at one of my confer-ences this whole week, and when we're not working and helping other people, we're going go swimming in the evening, we'll have breakfast together;" this part of the legacy I want to leave for them. I love being loved by people, but I adore being loved by my children, looked up to by them. I love it. I look up to them. They teach me so much.

The legacy I want to leave behind is being a true servant leader who lights people's world up. I created an acronym (LIGHHT):
Learn It
Implement it
Grow It
Hone it
Help just being an example you will touch those around you
Teach it to inspire change in others' lives
I want my legacy to be a light long after I'm gone. To just be known as Atarah Wright, a great mom and devoted wife with a phenomenal mission to financially educate the masses.

Woody Woodward

Woody Woodward dropped out of high school at age 16, was a millionaire by 26 and flat broke by age 27. After clawing his way out of financial ruin he built four different multi-million dollar companies before he turned 40. Through overcoming this adversity Mr. Woodward has become a best-selling author of fifteen books about turning tragedy into triumph. Having interviewed over 2,500 people around the world for his research, he is the pioneer and founder of *Your Emotional Fingerprint*™. Understanding this cutting edge human technology allows one to strip back the layers of excuses and build a proper foundation for mass achievement in one's personal life, relationships and career. Emotional Fingerprint was chosen as one of the leading techniques to be presented to the United Nations to assist them in reaching their millennial goals.

His latest project is inspiring entrepreneurs with M.O.N.E.Y. Matrix™ daily videos that help them reach their goals, make more money and find fulfillment in their careers. He has shared his cutting edge techniques on ABC, CBS, NBC, FOX and Forbes.

Contact Info:
www.GetMoneyMatrix.com
www.MeetWoody.com

Shannon:

According to Forbes Magazine, real estate is one of the top three ways that people become wealthy. As a real estate expert, why do you feel that this is the case?

Woody:

Real estate is the only investment I know of where you have a tangible, physical product that, even if the market goes down, you can still use. Yes, you can say stocks are tangible, but in reality they're not. Yes, you can lease them out, you can do calls and you can do puts on them, but with real estate, even if the market crashes, you can physically rent that property. You get a tax write-off if you are renting the property; so to me, real estate has always been, looking back in history, one of the top ways to generate revenue.

Shannon:

Do you have an opinion on whether commercial real estate or residential real estate is a better investment?

Woody:

I have friends who do both. I personally have always done residential. As for my friends who do commercial real estate it adds a zero to their net worth. If you're going to make a hundred thousand dollars on flipping a residential property, you'll make about a million flipping a commercial property; so it's the same game, just bigger numbers. If you have the resources to do it, most billionaires do it in commercial property, not residential. A lot of millionaires do residential property.

Shannon:

How hard is it to get started in residential real estate if you don't have a lot of money?

Woody:

That's the great thing about residential versus commercial; it doesn't take hardly anything with residential. Nowadays, you can still put down 3 percent or 5 percent on a home to buy it and then flip it, or to let it appreciate and sell it in the future and make additional revenue by leasing it, or there are a lot of different techniques where you can do owner financing. Owner financing is when the seller can't sell a home, maybe it's a bad market, and they're willing to carry that note for you; so in essence, the seller becomes the bank and you're buying it directly from the seller. You then still have all the legal rights to that property, so you can rent it out, you can fix it up, you can sell it; you can do whatever you want, as long as the seller's paid in full when you sell that home.

Shannon:

When the seller's paid in full, how does that benefit them if they're the bank? How do they buy another house?

Woody:

There is only one of two reasons why a seller will finance, in my experience. First is that they have enough income on their own, but they're happy just to sell it because they want to get a higher interest rate. Right now, if you put your money in the bank, you're going to get maybe 1 or 1.5 percent. If they carry the note on that home for you, they can charge you 5, 7, even 10 percent, so they're making more money on their own money, so they become a bank.

The other reason is that sometimes in a bad market they just can't sell a home. Let's say they owe $200,000 on a home and the home's only worth $175,000, so they physically can't sell it unless they come up with the $25,000 difference; so they'll carry their loan for you, and then as the market changes and goes back up and the home's worth $250,000, you can then sell it and keep that extra $50,000 since you bought it for $200,000. Then they are happy because now they get their $200,000 out that they already owe their bank, and it becomes a little win-win.

Shannon:

When you're actually looking for homes in a down market situation where people are upside down in their homes, do you look at the location? Do you look at the future projections for businesses, neighborhoods, etc.?

Woody:

Absolutely. The number one thing that you hear people always talk about with real estate, the number one technique, is location, location, location. I've had friends who have literally bought corner lots and then they heard that Walmart was coming across the street. This happened to a friend of mind in California who bought the lot for $150,000 and had the owner carry the note. Six months later Walmart announced that they were building across the street. His lot went from $150,000 to $500,000 literally overnight. He would be able to sell that and take that money. Now he can play in the commercial business on a little bit larger level.

Most investor works the same way. You make a little bit, you turn that money over. It's really called compounding interest where you take your principle and your interest and then you roll it over again into the next property. There's also a great tax benefit to that as well. You don't have to pay tax on that money as long as you're rolling it over in to a property of equal or higher value.

Shannon:

What do you think is the number one mistake that an individual makes when buying their first investment property?

Woody:

The number one reason why people make mistakes on their first investment property is they don't have a mentor. They don't have someone to follow. They don't have someone that can show them the right thing to do. They just hear their buddies doing it, they go out and they buy a home, but they haven't done all the certification, they haven't verified that this property's not going to have termite issues or meth issues, or something else that could really hurt them. They think, "Oh, it's a good deal, I can buy that and make a ton of money." The benefit to real estate is there's tons of people and there's tons of organizations out there that have already done it a thousand times, so connect with them. Join an investment club, join a company that does education, and then they'll help you limit your potential risk.

Shannon:

How have your mentors in real estate investing helped you to navigate pitfalls?

Woody:

We don't know what we don't know, and every deal has a potential problem, and every deal tends to really have a problem. I'm in the middle of a transaction right now where the home had to be lifted. We knew that there were some cracks in the foundation, but we weren't sure; so before we actually took ownership and before we actually even wrote the contract, we had an engineer come out. The only reason I did that is my mentor recommended, "You know what Woody, if you've got cracks in your foundation that are larger than average, hire an engineer. Spend the six, seven, eight hundred dollars. You'll save hundreds of thousands of dollars of potential losses for a small investment", so we did that and it ended up costing the seller $75,000 to raise that foundation. Had we bought that home not knowing that, we'd be out $75,000, so an $800 investment saved me $75,000.

Now, after the home was raised, we paid another $400 for an inspector to go out and verify absolutely everything. What he did is he pulled off all of the insulation in the basement and found another crack that we didn't know about, so now we're having another company come out and verify that crack because you can see daylight through the foundation. That's never good. You never want to see daylight in the foundation.

They're coming out to fix that. Once again, the seller will have to pay that and we won't.

Shannon:

How do you help other people learn more about real estate?

Woody:

Everybody has that friend who is in real estate. I'm that friend for my friends, and they will always ask me, "Woody what about this?" Or, "What about that transaction? What about that home you flipped?" What I like to do is just invite them to come along and take a look.

There's times where I'll take five of my friends and show them a house that I'm doing, show them the pitfalls and mistakes, and where's the benefit to changing it.

This one home, there is about $100,000 in equity from us just buying it right. I believe that when it comes to real estate, you make your money when you buy it, not when you sell it, so you have to buy it right.

Shannon:

You are obviously passionate about real estate. What actually inspired you to get into the industry?

Woody:

I grew up with my folks in a different generation where my dad was the traditional father who would always work and my mother would stay home. In the 80's when the market crashed and we didn't have a lot of money, it was a challenge, and so my mom became a realtor. She would list homes, so when I was very young, I'd go with my mom when she would go list a home. I'd walk through these homes and they were, to a kid, like a jungle gym. They were just so fascinating, and I grew up being exposed to real estate. I met some of the investors who my mom was selling for and it changed my life forever.

If you list a home as a typical realtor, you'll make 3 percent. The investor can make 10 to 20 percent. They're just taking the greater risk. The realtor doesn't have any risk. They have some advertising costs, but that's not a huge risk. The investor who bought the home, fixed it up, put new paint/carpet in, now is making $50,000, $100,000, $150,000 on a transaction. That blew my mind, and that was the second I knew I wanted to be in real estate.

Shannon:

What are some of the creative ways that you use now, or what is your favorite way to find a property to acquire a fix and flip?

Woody:

For me the best way to find property is to know your area, so back to location, location, location. The home that I'm buying right now, the one that had the sunken basement, we've been trying for two years to get this home. We've talked to the seller, he wouldn't sell it to us. Then low and behold we found out that he passed away, and then we went to his heirs, which was his older sister. Well, she's eighty-four years old. She doesn't want to deal with this property. She lives out of state, but because I was driving around, just driving by this one house that I've always wanted to acquire, I saw a car there. I knew he lived out of state. It was an investment property for him, so when I saw a car there, I just knocked on the door. And told them that because the home had been vacant for over three years, that's why it was neglected and the home sunk. Basically, I was able to get the home before it even went on the market.

Had they taken the time to invest in the property, to fix it up, and then to sell it, I would've been out of the loop. So to me the best technique is, take an area, a geographical area that you know well and trust, and then master it. Know every house. You can pull titles. You can find out when people are delinquent. You can ask them to buy the home before it goes into foreclosure. There are so many techniques to save yourself time because it's trying to find that jewel in the rough. It's always hard to find, but when you find one, you can pull out fifty to a hundred grand.

Shannon:
How do you decide if you are going to fix and flip a home or buy and hold it for rental income?

Woody:
If I'm in a financial position where I can hold it and I can keep it long-term and I believe a certain area geographically is going to go up in value, then I will hold it. I have done holds in the past, but on the fix and flips, those are the ones that give you large pops. Wealthy people, I believe, get wealthy by the large pops–fifty grand, a hundred grand, two hundred and fifty grand pops. I've made $200,000 on a house in thirty days. I can't save that much money myself, I can't save my way to wealth, and I don't believe most people can. You look at CEOs who have large stock options and a buyout takes place; they

get a large pop of millions of dollars, so to create massive wealth, you've got to have large pops.

Well, as soon as you've had enough large pops where you've got a good nest egg, now you can afford to buy one, hold it, and if a renter does not pay, you can afford to make that monthly payment. I don't believe in being house poor. If you own a bunch of properties but you can't fix up the yard or you can't take a vacation, I call that being house poor. You may have a million dollars in real estate, but you can't afford to take a vacation, then you don't have the life that real estate's designed to give you.

Shannon:
I'd like to go back to when you said you saw the car and you just knocked on the door. Tell me how that conversation went?

Woody:
It's very simple. You can tell when somebody is stressed. You can see it on their face. This woman looked bewildered. This is the first time she had seen this home after her brother passed. She didn't want that property. She lives two thousand miles away. She wants nothing to do with this property. I asked her, "You know what, I've been watching this home for two years. Are you the new owner? She said, "Yeah, my brother passed, and now I have inherited this home." I said, "Well, what is your intention? Do you want to sell the home, or do you want to keep it and rent it out? What would you like to do?" "Oh my gosh, I just want to sell this home," she replied, so I gave her an offer on the spot. She turned it down. I waited about a month. I kept checking on the home. I saw them doing yard work trying to fix it up. I went back to her, I said, "You know what, are you by chance interested in selling the home yet?" At that point, she was, because she just realized how much work it was going to be to fix it up.

You have to understand that if someone is going to sell you a house at a discount than what it should be going for, that means there's inherently something wrong with the home. Either it needs new carpet, or they had pets in there, or it smells. It's been neglected. Things are broken. So when you're looking for a fix and flip, they're never in perfect condition, otherwise they'd get top of the retail value. People who have these homes don't want them because they know how much it's going to cost to fix it, and that was the case with her, so it was really easy to buy it from her, to take that pressure and stress off of her.

Shannon:

Do you think that you can have real estate success being a one- man- show, or do you think that most people need to have a team?

Woody:

When I say I'm a one-man show I don't want to imply that I don't have a team and I don't work with other people because that's not true. I don't have employees that I pay that help me run my company, but I have a network of people that I work with. In real estate you cannot be successful without a network of people. It's impossible. You need to know a title guy, a realtor. You need to know an appraiser. There are so many moving parts in real estate, you need to have a group of people you work with.

When it comes to education, I go back to that saying, "We don't know what we don't know." Create an environment and a network, facilitate a mastermind, put people who are in real estate in the same room and you will expedite your knowledge. You'll expedite your learning curves. It is crucial that you spend time with a team of people who have your best interest in mind to make you successful.

Shannon:

What is your favorite investment strategy when the market is good and homes are selling quickly?

Woody:

In California in 2005 when the market was just exploding and homes were appreciating at 30 percent a year, if you bought a home for $400,000, in a year it was going for a $520,000, so in that market we were buying homes that weren't even built yet. When a new subdivision was under construction we would put down $5,000. Homes would take six months to nine months to build. By the time we bought that home and moved into it, we already had $60,000 to $80,000 of appreciation; so in an up market my favorite thing to do is speculation. Know an area, know where the parks and schools are being built, buy homes that are under construction so that you can flip them as soon as you close on them.

Shannon:

When you look at everything that you do in your life, your real estate investing career, your entrepreneurial adventures, and your life married with children, what legacy do you want to leave?

Woody:

I want my children and the people that I have the opportunity to come in contact with to realize that they can change. Regardless of your past, regardless of where you started, you can change. I believe real estate is one of the greatest agents for change. It allows someone, even an uneducated person like myself, to learn something, to master something, and then to make a very good income with it.

My legacy is that I want people to realize they can do it. That's the bottom line, that they can have their own life, that they can change, that they can become who they want to become regardless of their background.

As my wife would say, "We are just borrowing it for a time before the next generation borrows it." Since we don't take anything with us, I would want my legacy to be the impact I have had on my relationships. There is no doubt my life has been better because of the lives of others. I would like to do the same for someone else.